PANHARD
ARMOURED CAR
1961 onwards (AML 60, AML 90 and Eland)

COVER IMAGE: Eland Mark 7.

(Artwork by Pierre Lowe Victor)

Dedication
To Daniel and Ysobel

First published in February 2019

A catalogue record for this book is available from the British Library.

ISBN 978 1 78521 194 2

Library of Congress control no. 2018938903

Published by Haynes Publishing,
Sparkford, Yeovil, Somerset BA22 7JJ, UK.
Tel: 01963 440635
Int. tel: +44 1963 440635
Website: www.haynes.com

Haynes North America Inc.,
859 Lawrence Drive, Newbury Park,
California 91320, USA.

Printed in Malaysia.

Acknowledgements

The author wishes to express his sincere thanks to the all those who have kindly contributed to this history of the Panhard AML and Eland armoured cars: Richard Allport, Ryan Anthony, Tony Ballinger, Sam van den Berg, Tom Bunim, Hans Burger, Jose Luis Calvo, Dirk Coetzee, Rea Cullivan, Haim Danon, Basil Duke-Norris, Barrimore England-Davis, Kieran Flynn, Christopher F. Foss, John French, Ofer Fridman, Chris Geldenhuys, Mark Goller, Paul Haley, Kyle Harmse, Helmoed-Römer Heitman, John Hopkins, Sir Roy Jackson, Heinrich Janzen, Martin Klotz, Hans Kriek, Danie Malan, William Marshall, Patrick Mercer, Shaul Nagar, Andre du Plessis, Nel van Rensberg, Mark Richardson, M.P. Robinson, Thomas Seignon, H.W. Short, Toon Slabbert, Richard Stickland, William Surmon, Dick Taylor, Pierre Touzin, André Venter, Pierre Lowe Victor, Lou van Vuuren, David Williams, Steven J. Zaloga, Koos Zietsman.

Unless otherwise credited, all the photographs in this volume are courtesy of the following sources: the Archives of Société Panhard; Arme Blindé Cavalerie; Musée des Blindés, Saumur; Collection Claude Dubarry; Collection Christian Dumont; Collection Thomas Seignon.

Simon Dunstan, Suffolk, 2018

PANHARD

ARMOURED CAR

1961 onwards (AML 60, AML 90 and Eland)

Enthusiasts' Manual

Insights into the design and combat use of the 'Universal Armoured Car' that has been in service with armies worldwide

Simon Dunstan

Contents

OPPOSITE The Patrouille de France aerobatic team flies over the Arc de Triomphe and a formation of Panhard AML 60 armoured cars during the Bastille Day parade of 14 July 1969. *(Getty Images)*

Foreword

Lieutenant-Général Martin Klotz

Général de Corps d'Armée (2S), Officier de la Légion d'Honneur,
Commandeur de l'Ordre National du Mérite, Croix de Valeur Militaire (two citations)

L'auto-mitrailleuse légère, un mythe devenu réalité!
(The light armoured car – a myth becomes reality!)

As well as an armoured fighting vehicle, the AML became a mythical creature and a legendary weapon in the French Arme Blindée Cavalerie. For over 40 years this diminutive vehicle contributed to France's defence as well as to her overseas operations – most notably in Africa and in Lebanon. A legendary weapon deserves a suitable homage and this remarkable work by Simon Dunstan tells the AML's complex story.

My own association with the AML began as a young lieutenant when I had the privilege of being assigned command of an AML platoon in 1983. More than any other job in the cavalry in those days, the command of an AML platoon was a young officer's dream. The light cavalry in those days consisted of only four AML regiments, and securing a command in one of these was very much dependent on how well one had performed during the Saumur cavalry officer's course. Besides, the garrisons of these four regiments were prized as fine postings indeed!

An AML platoon comprised five armoured cars, of which two were armed with 90mm guns and three with 60mm mortars. We also had four Hotchkiss Jeeps and a supply truck, giving the platoon commander a total of ten vehicles. These ten vehicles and the combinations in which they could operate gave a lieutenant a wide range of tactical options. The AML gave an unsurpassed firepower to weight ratio at that time, a feat that has not since been surpassed anywhere. These 5-tonne vehicles, especially the AML 90, were unparalleled for the formidable firepower they offered. Never before had such a light vehicle carried so much firepower.

The simplicity of the AML, both in design and in operation, was also remarkable. Its crews could make minor repairs to their damaged vehicles easily and breakdowns seldom prevented the fulfilment of missions. It was reliable and its crewmen were readily trained. Obviously, at such a light weight the AML was not heavily armoured. We tended to refer to the AML simply as a 'car', rather than as an armoured car. The compact size and low silhouette of the little Panhard was an important component of its crew protection, making it a diminutive target. It was hard to hit an AML moving across country.

I also got a chance to see the value of the AML in overseas operations during 1985 and 1986. In operations in Lebanon the AML proved itself the ideal weapon system for advancing through the narrow streets and lanes of south Lebanese villages. An AML 90's gun could fire high explosive or hollow charge HEAT rounds accurately to some 2,000m and represented a serious deterrent to any potential enemy.

In the French Army's operations in Africa, conducted from the early 1960s right up to the end of the 20th century, the AML figured prominently. This marvellous armoured vehicle could be deployed rapidly from France by air and was so easy to support in the field that we could describe it as a weapon with a 'small logistic footprint'. With its firepower and the tactics we used, AMLs counted as highly on the African battlefields as tanks might have elsewhere! One has to wonder how many terrible situations were averted by the arrival of an AML platoon; how many times AMLs served as force multipliers for small French units to dissuade insurgent attacks or how many civilian lives were saved. In Africa the AML was often the decisive weapon, one that belied the very small numbers of French AFVs available at any one time.

Heir to the 'automitrailleuses de découverte' of the pre-1940 era, the Panhard AML permitted several generations of French cavalrymen to live up to the elements of the old cavalry ethos held so dearly in the *Arme Blanche*. These were the audacity that permitted the cavalryman to disrupt an enemy with the element of surprise ; add to this the spirit of teamwork forged in an armoured vehicle crew that allows them to act effortlessly as one in the chaos of battle. Finally we cannot forget the panache and elegance of the small units that employed these vehicles. Panhard AMLs were the ideal weapon for cavalrymen who were the heirs of the horsemen of long ago. This cavalry spirit transcended the ages and survives today in the men who served on the AML, a machine which has passed into legend and that left its mark on recent history.

Et par Saint Georges ... vive la cavalerie!

Author's preface

AML: the Universal Armoured Car

At the outset of the Second World War a group of First World War tank designers offered their services to the British government to develop a tank that would address the perceived conditions of a contemporary European battlefield. The result was the TOG 1 and TOG 2 that derived their designations from the sobriquet given to the venerable group of designers – 'The Old Gang'. During the 1960s and 1970s there grew up a group of armour enthusiasts keen to record both the history and the contemporary role of armoured fighting vehicles (AFVs). Names such as Christopher F. Foss, Professor Richard M. Ogorkiewicz, Raymond Surlémont, Pierre Touzin and the present author all cut their teeth on such AFVs as the Panhard AML and their works are reflected in this volume. They are 'The Old Gang' of today's armour publishing world, so it is highly encouraging that a new generation of academics and writers are pursuing this field as well. These include Rea Cullivan, Barrimore England-Davis, Kyle Harmse, M.P. Robinson and Thomas Seignon, respectively

BELOW The primary role of any reconnaissance vehicle is to gain information of enemy dispositions through stealth or, in a final resort, through fire and movement, with crews using terrain and natural features to allow observation without disclosing their own position to hostile fire.

from the USA, Britain, South Africa, Canada and France. All contributed considerably to this Haynes Enthusiasts' Manual for that is what they are – true enthusiasts. Sadly, most of the contemporary armour publications are devoted to AFVs sporting white stars or black crosses so many truly outstanding AFVs never get the recognition they deserve and the Panhard Automitrailleuse Légère is a classic case in point.

The Panhard AML represented a highly successful commercial venture borne out of the French Army's desire to produce a weapon similar in size to the British Ferret, with the firepower of a larger and heavier weapon system following the lessons of the war in Algeria. The HB 60mm breech-loading mortar was a fine weapon for local fire support that surpassed the performance of the 37mm-gunned M8 Greyhound, and the 90mm CN-90-F1 far surpassed the performance of the 75mm gun carried by the M24 light tank. These American 37mm and 75mm guns were the benchmark weapons widely used by the French Army during the 1950s both in Indochina and subsequently in Algeria. The Panhard AML then went on to eclipse completely the British Ferret scout car and Saladin armoured car on the international arms market in the 1970s. It became the AFV of choice on the African continent for two decades, where it still serves in several armies. Its story is also particular in the fact that it represents one of the few private companies in France to market a weapon system successfully in an industry dominated by the state run DEFA and its successor DTAT. While this was not possible without government support, it was an outstanding achievement for Panhard – a company whose very existence was jeopardised when the Algerian campaign abruptly ended in 1962 and French Army orders were dramatically reduced.

This remarkable story recounts the development of a French armoured car family that usurped the British out of one of the most lucrative sectors of the armaments industry for the Third World governments seeking to entrench themselves behind newly formed national armies. As often as not, these regimes were averse to buying, or were unable to buy, American AFVs because of political factors,

or because nobody else offered anything like the balance of qualities available in the AML for a comparable price. Britain had dominated this market in the late 1950s and early 1960s with the Ferret and Saladin. The Anglo-Saxon arms producers developed comparatively few armoured car designs after 1965, besides the undistinguished Fox. The need for the wheeled armoured car in the worlds' armies, a relatively cheap, and always versatile, weapon system, did not disappear when British and American designers saw the future of their armoured reconnaissance forces in light aluminium armoured tracked vehicles in the 1960s. It was Panhard that seized and filled this void in the arms markets throughout the 1970s and into the 1980s. Thereafter, France remained the leading producer of wheeled reconnaissance vehicles with designs such as the Panhard Sagaie, the AMX 10RC up to today's innovative Panhard Crab and Nexter Jaguar – both foremost exemplars of the true reconnaissance vehicle.

Of all the foreign customers, South Africa stands out as the country that carried the torch for the AML with their indigenous development and manufacture of the Eland that continued in production into the 1990s. The Eland won its spurs during the Border War in South West Africa and Angola during much of the 1970s and 1980s when it gained a fearsome reputation among friend and foe alike. Thanks to its innate mechanical reliability and the can-do attitude of its crews and the formation commanders, the Eland was employed as an offensive weapon when first deployed in combat during Operation 'Savannah' in 1975 (see Chapter 7). It proved highly significant within the overall success of the campaign. It thus set the scene for all subsequent armour operations in the Border War up to Operation 'Askari' in 1974 when the Eland was effectively superseded by the Ratel ICV. But in the words of Major General Toon Slabbert who, as a major, led the charge of the Elands in Operation 'Savannah': 'The Eland was the best armoured car in the world'. Both the AML and the Eland fought across the length and breadth of Africa from Morocco to Mozambique; from Kenya to Chad; from Gabon to Angola: it was an African battle winner *sans pareil*.

Introduction

The role of reconnaissance

Brig Gen Chris Gildenhuys; Southern Cross Medal, Military Merit Medal
formerly Director of Operations, Joint Operations Division, South African National Defence Force

In military operations, reconnaissance, also known by some as scouting, is the exploration outside an area occupied by friendly forces to gain information about the terrain (natural features) and other activities, mainly that of the enemy. Since the earliest days of warfare, reconnaissance troops were tasked to discover the dispositions and strengths of enemy forces in the area and, if possible, also the intentions of the opposing forces. Such information had to be relayed to the force commander at best possible speed.

A key performance area for the conduct of successful military operations is intelligence. Intelligence is the product of processed information, which on the other hand is often obtained by means of reconnaissance. In both offensive and defensive operations an element of the main force would be tasked to conduct reconnaissance. Secondary spin-offs of this force's performance could be liaison (with flanking forces), security (for the main force not to be surprised) and sometimes even deception. Because speed of action has always been a requirement, the reconnaissance task used to be carried out on horseback until the late 19th century and early years of the 20th century. Since the dawn of the age of mechanisation, these tasks have been performed mainly by armoured vehicles due to their inherent mobility and speed of communications. Reconnaissance can also be done by air, special operations way behind enemy lines and other clandestine means.

It is not a matter of performing reconnaissance or not. It is generally accepted that time spent on reconnaissance is seldom wasted – or is considered time well spent. Reconnaissance during all types of operations is thus of the essence. Only by means of effective reconnaissance can information be gathered from which intelligence is derived and thereby workable operational plans can be drafted and ultimately executed.

From days gone by until today, there are two main approaches to reconnaissance – the first is to perform as clandestinely as possible by means of stealth and the second to gain information by means of active combat, in other words fighting for information. A classic example of the latter is the offensive actions of the United States' 1st Battalion, 64th Armor during the operation into western Baghdad in April 2003 during Operation 'Desert Storm'. This reconnaissance-offensive was launched to prepare for the 3rd Mechanised Infantry

BELOW The AML 90 was a compact vehicle with a height of 2.07m (6ft 9in) whereas the AML 60 was just 5ft 11in – about the same as a standing man. Combined with a top speed of 60kmh (37mph) it presented a difficult target to engage on the battlefield, while its firepower was exceptional for a vehicle of such size.

Division's advance on the Iraqi capital. The eventually successful mission was planned as a battalion-sized reconnaissance-in-force to determine the composition, strength and disposition of the enemy's defences and ultimately its will to fight.

Both stealthy operations as well as fighting for information have a place in doctrine and tactics. The operational situation will dictate the decision to go stealth or otherwise. The lighter and less noisy, the stealthier it is. The heavier, more aggressive, the better prepared for combat, in other words having an ability to fight for information. And off course the heavier the force the bigger the demand on logistics.

Armies across the world have always been faced by the question of how to design and structure its reconnaissance forces and how to equip them. In the German Bundeswehr reconnaissance forces are organised and structured in units at division and brigade level and are mainly equipped with both wheeled and heavy tracked equipment. In the British Army units are grouped at corps level and equipped with light wheeled armoured vehicles, the reason being that its mission is to collect information only and that observation thus enjoys priority over combat.

Since the 1970s, the French Army has been conventional and nuclear-warfare orientated and employs equipped corps level units to do passive observation but also be prepared to engage the enemy. However, it has also structured and equipped lighter forces, the so-called Défense Operationelle du Territoire, to operate in the interior in close cooperation with police, civilian defence and military reserves for which the Panhard AML was primarily developed.

The United States' large, light-wheeled and tracked armoured cavalry regiments have similar missions as for the British and French. They are equipped with both wheeled lighter armoured vehicles (LAVs) and tracked Bradley cavalry fighting vehicles, as well as helicopters under the formation reconnaissance commander.

The Russians (and former Soviet Union forces) also have reconnaissance units at division and regimental level with its mission to

BELOW An Eland Mk 7 engages a target during a night-firing exercise on the de Brug ranges near the South African Armoured Corps School of Armour at Bloemfontein in Free State.

collect tactical information through observation, thereby avoiding combat if possible. The light-amphibious tracked erstwhile PT-76, among others forms the core element of these forces. Their reconnaissance battalions can furthermore be reinforced by combined arms, light aviation and paratroopers. Its missions include the fixing of hostile nuclear batteries, detection of large enemy concentrations and to prepare for the commitment of their major combat units.

The South African Army had vast experience in mobile warfare and operations. It operated with mainly wheeled armoured vehicles in northern Namibia and the southern parts of Angola due to its involvement in the so-called Bush War of the 1970s, '80s and '90s. The all-drive four-wheeled Eland armoured car, born out of the French Panhard AML, and later the Ratel 6 x 6 armoured fighting vehicle, played a significant role in reconnaissance and in all types of offensive and defensive operations.

The French Panhard was 'South Africanised' in the 1960s to become the Eland (named after a large indigenous antelope) armoured car. For some three decades the 6-tonne Eland has proven itself as a stalwart of South Africa's armour capabilities. Two regular force armoured car units, 1 and 2 Special Service Battalions, as well as several citizen force reserve units, effectively deployed the Eland in counter-insurgency operations and later also in pre-emptive operations during raids into southern Angola. Its main task in northern Namibia was reconnaissance and patrolling of roads, border lines, key points and the protection of local inhabitants from insurgents. Thick sandy roads posed a serious challenge to Eland drivers as they were forced to change almost non-stop through the lower gears at high engine revolutions – causing a high-pitched noise that sometimes gave away the position or movement of friendly forces.

The real test for Eland and its crews, however, came in 1975 during Operation 'Savannah' in the central parts of Angola. Not only did South African National Defence Force (SANDF) battlegroups advance at record tempos with Eland squadrons and troops leading, but Eland also encountered far heavier and better protected and armed enemy armour. In the process Eland unwittingly adopted

the role of a light tank, a role well beyond the reconnaissance function it was originally destined for. Notwithstanding this unusual demand, were the young, adventurous and well-trained crews able to destroy many a target by means of the very reliable and accurate 90mm quick-firing gun's anti-tank (HEAT) and high-explosive (HE) ammunition.

With the introduction of the South African designed, developed and manufactured Rooikat 8 x 8 in the beginning of the '90s, the trustworthy Eland was (sadly) decommissioned – a decision that many would argue was premature. The combination of Eland and its battle-hardened crews gained a reputation second to none as it was a formidable combination and force to be reckoned with.

Over time the nature of the battlefield has changed – from a force-on-force symmetrical set-up to a more asymmetrical nature where the threat is somehow difficult to define and to be located. In the process equipment such as armoured vehicles have also been revolutionised to provide for the best possible mobility, protection and firepower. However, reconnaissance remains a prerequisite for successful military operations, irrespective the nature of the battlefield.

The South African Army is currently busy developing a multi-roled capability providing for a light armoured as well as a reconnaissance role suitable for the asymmetrical battlefield where both high mobility as well as high intensity operations may be conducted. The highly mobile wheeled light armoured vehicles will be fitted with advanced technology surveillance equipment and sensors.

So, be it for use in purely conventional operations or operations other than war (OOTW), such as peace-keeping operations, armoured units, wheeled or tracked, have a significant role to play in reconnaissance. Gathering information through either stealthy observation and actions, or by fighting, or a combination thereof, is of the essence. The force commander needs to understand the nature of the terrain and other natural features but mainly the composition, strength, disposition and intentions of the opposing forces to conduct successful military operations. He can only achieve that through the conduct of effective reconnaissance.

Chapter One

A century of Panhard

As one of the world's first automobile manufacturers, the company of Panhard and Levassor soon produced vehicles and engines for the military in a tradition that was to last for over 100 years. From the beginning, Panhard armoured cars were world leaders with such outstanding designs as the AMD 35, the EBR 75 and Automitrailleuse Légère or AML – the latter being the most commercially successful of them all.

OPPOSITE The Automitrailleuse de Découverte Modele 1935 or Panhard 178 was a highly effective armoured car in the early years of the Second World War, used by the French cavalry and later the German Army. *(Steven Zaloga)*

There are many claimants to the invention of the internal combustion engine. The British engineer, Edward Butler, constructed the first such petrol-powered engine in 1884 and he was the first to coin the term 'petroleum spirit' or 'petrol'. By the end of the decade the technology was well established as a means to power a four-wheel carriage that became known as the automobile. Manufacturers sprang up across the industrialised world, including the company of Panhard et Levassor in Paris, after they obtained a licence to build the engine devised by the contemporary German engineer, Gottlieb Daimler.

Panhard et Levassor was the first company to introduce the concept of the modern car with four wheels, a front-mounted engine with rear-wheel drive, steered by a wheel instead of a handle, and a clutch pedal to operate a chain-driven gearbox. The Système Panhard became the basic configuration of automobiles for many decades to come.

As with most armies of the period, the French General Staff soon came to realise the potential of the motor car for greater mobility on the battlefield as an adjunct to the horse, which remained the principal means of transport and exploitation. In early 1898 the French Army proposed a comparative trial of the automobiles produced by the country's various established manufacturers. At this time there were just 1,600 automobiles in the whole of France. The six entrants in the trial were recorded as two Panhard-Levassors, two Peugeots, and two Maison Parisiennes. On 18 March 1898, War Minister General Jean-Baptiste Billot, signed the first purchase order for two Panhard automobiles for the French Army – it was the beginning of a tradition that continues to this day.

On account of its four-cylinder sleeve-valve engine, the Panhards proved to be suitably reliable and more orders followed as mechanisation began in earnest across contemporary armies. In 1904 the first military specified types were purchased from Panhard, including a 15hp Landaulette that served as a staff car and a 24hp Voiture Rapide de Reconnaissance. The latter had a wide range of applications in a modern army. The idea

BELOW The Panhard et Levassor Landaulette Mle A1 of 1898 was the precursor of the modern motor car with Système Panhard.

BELOW RIGHT The first Panhard vehicle sold to the French Army in 1898 was essentially a civilian automobile that was employed by the headquarters of the 70th Infantry Brigade. It was driven by M. Journu, a reservist who became the first military chauffeur in the French Army, seen here grasping the steering handle of his vehicle.

of a mobile detachment supplementing cavalry operations was attractive to several forward-thinking officers, but it was already obvious that it was vulnerable to small-arms weapons as were horses. Such a car could not be defended with anything less than a machine-gun, since rifle fire could not be accurately delivered from a moving car. At the time, French cavalry brigades included a horse-mounted machine-gun section and it was not long before the idea of mounting the machine-gun on a Panhard reconnaissance car was put to the test.

Capitaine Henry-Francois Genty, an automobile enthusiast officer who saw the combustion engine as one of the great future weapons of war, had already purchased his own automobile in 1904. Genty, who regularly took part in the nascent motorsport racing events of the day under the assumed name of La Touloubre, was a man ahead of his time. Genty had been interested in previous years in expanding the military use of the bicycle, and wrote essays on the impact of advances in mobility on modern armies. He was assigned to command the new three-car artillery utility vehicle section and its maintenance detachment at Vincennes in 1900. In 1905 Capitaine Genty obtained permission to test the Panhard 24hp four-seat reconnaissance car with a Hotchkiss 8mm machine-gun mounting fitted. The Panhard 24hp was a four-seat car, weighed some 1,200kg, and was capable of speeds of 70kmh on a good road, with a range of 250km. It featured a wooden and steel chassis like many vehicles of its time, and its Hotchkiss 8mm could be fitted to a post-type mount along the vehicle centreline either pointing forward, or on a second rear-facing mounting. The vehicle carried some 2,100 rounds of ammunition in nine boxes, a tripod to permit the use of the machine-gun dismounted and a telescope to permit surveillance of the surroundings.

Capitaine Genty employed the Panhard in the 1905 manoeuvres held in the Aube district under the command of the 1ère Division de Cavalerie. During the ten-day operation, the Panhard motored for over 1,500km. No mechanical incidents seem to have been

ABOVE Captain Henry-Francois Genty sits at the wheel of the first armed Panhard automobile (top photograph) in the Panhard works at Avenue d'Ivry in Paris and (below) during the 1905 manoeuvres held in the Aube district under the command of the 1ère Division de Cavalerie.

reported in this time. To paraphrase the positive report of the division commander:

'The auto-mitrailleur [sic] renders a useful service to the cavalry division, especially at the outset of an operation. The vehicle never tires like a horse does, and it can be used in the attack or as a reconnaissance vehicle. It is ideal to employ in a coup de main, where a crossroads, a bridge or a section of railway must be taken or destroyed. It can be used as a liaison vehicle, or as a supply carrier to support raiding cavalry.'

Genty spent the next few years working out tactics for the use of armed cars, and he wrote several works for the army detailing what types of tools and supplies were needed by automobile detachments to permit them to operate autonomously. The weapon enthused Genty and he became well known within the army as an expert on automobile warfare. All the same, the army was slow to view the armed car as a weapon that could be adopted in numbers, which slowly changed after its first use in combat.

In Morocco in July 1907, local rebels massacred Europeans in Casablanca. This fomented a general insurrection and the army was sent to restore order. General Lyautey was sent from France to take command and he demanded the automitrailleuse, still a single prototype and known as the Panhard-Genty after its exponent, be sent to Morocco. Capitaine Genty arrived himself in North Africa on 18 December 1907 with his armed Panhard-Genty 24hp and a small detachment. How this vehicle would perform, with rear-wheel drive

and without any special modifications for use off roads, was unknown. The Panhard negotiated seemingly impassable terrain in pursuit of insurgents, crossing the Kiss with surprising ease. The car proved to be an ideal weapon for counter-insurgency and the rebels were soon terrified of it.

Genty would write: 'I had to wonder if the terrain in Morocco would permit the same excellent results we had seen in France, but soon enough my expectations were exceeded by both man and machine.'

Genty's idea of highly mobile firepower was applied enthusiastically against the rebels in Morocco; two more Panhard 24hp auto mitrailleuses (armoured cars) were converted for the army and sent to North Africa. General Bailloud warmly supported the tactical effectiveness of using the then incredible firepower of the automitrailleuses. The insurgents feared these cars and called them La Maboula. The automitrailleuse detachment saw incredibly hard use for the next few years in the rocky and dusty Moroccan wastes, but the 24hp chassis proved durable (and remained serviceable

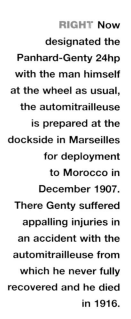

RIGHT Now designated the Panhard-Genty 24hp with the man himself at the wheel as usual, the automitrailleuse is prepared at the dockside in Marseilles for deployment to Morocco in December 1907. There Genty suffered appalling injuries in an accident with the automitrailleuse from which he never fully recovered and he died in 1916.

LEFT The three original automitrailleuses were produced on the Panhard 1904 chassis while the second batch in 1909 featured an all-steel chassis with the first vestiges of armour plate for greater protection.

for many more years). In 1908, Genty and one of his men were injured in a terrible accident involving one of the cars, and the captain had to endure a long and difficult convalescence for the rest of his days.

In 1909 Lyautey supported a request from Genty for the army to provide him with an additional pair of 24hp automitrailleuses, the existing vehicles having been repaired at a cost of 4,000 Francs and having been returned to Genty's detachment with 6mm armour plate mudguards added, the first semblance of an armoured body provided for these vehicles. The new order produced a quandary for Panhard: the three original 24hp cars were based on the Panhard 1904 chassis model, which was no longer in production in 1909, and so the two new cars featured an all-steel chassis.

The second order showed Panhard as an admirably responsive supplier: the French Army's second order for automitrailleuses was received on 28 April 1909 and work started that very day on the first chassis. Panhard's staff worked double shifts in the knowledge that insurrection was raging in Morocco, and so the first hand-built car was completed in three weeks. The second car was ready a fortnight later and the third by the middle of June. The three new cars were delivered and armed and were sent immediately across the Mediterranean and into action.

Ten more Model 1909 24hp automitrailleuses were built that year to fill army orders and all were still in service as automitrailleuses in 1914. By the end of 1914, 2,000 separate government orders for Panhard products had been placed. The army ordered aircraft and vehicle engines, weapons components, and of course complete vehicles of several types. The navy ordered engines for submarines from Panhard as well. Thanks to Capitaine Genty, Panhard had been noticed by the army, and the company had discovered a true vocation. For Panhard's ambitious foray into the world of mobile warfare however, the war came as an anticlimax.

Despite the promise of the automitrailleuse, the Panhard company's light armoured vehicles only played a minor role in the First World War. While the original 24hp cars came back from Morocco and served throughout on the Western Front (some receiving armoured bodies during the war), Panhard focused on selling staff cars and built the engines for the 400 St Chamond char d'assault during 1916–18. Peugeot, White and Renault cornered the armoured car market in France during the latter part of the war. Tragically the brilliant Capitaine Genty never recovered from the automobile accident in Morocco that left him semi-paralysed, and he died an invalid on 7 May 1916. He was posthumously awarded the honour of Officier de la Légion d'Honneur with the following citation: 'Exceptional war service in military automobiles. Badly wounded twice in combat in Africa while commanding a car and demonstrating the highest ideals of audacity and energy.'

What Genty might have achieved had he not been incapacitated in expanding the role of the armed automobile between 1909 and 1914 can only be imagined. It would be several years before Panhard regained a strong enough position to sell the army an armed (and by then armoured) vehicle.

The interwar Panhards

In 1922 Panhard renewed its efforts to construct a dedicated armoured car for the French Army. The army's Automilitrailleuse de Cavalerie Numéro 1 (AMC No 1) specification was a collaborative effort – in other words it required an armoured body constructed in a government arsenal and a chassis and powertrain supplied as a complete unit by a private manufacturer. The idea had its origins in wartime and was carried forward thereafter in the matter of turret design especially. The AMC No 1 resulted in an armoured body being designed by the Atelier de Vincennes. The contract was offered to Panhard if they could provide a suitable chassis and powertrain. A utility lorry chassis powered by a 20hp engine with rear wheel drive was proposed. The turret envisaged was identical to those carried by the Renault armoured car, with a 37mm SA-18 gun and an 8mm machine-gun mounted in opposite faces of the turret. A rearward-facing driver's position was provided, permitting the crew to disengage at speed as soon as contact was made when conducting a reconnaissance.

This first completely armoured Panhard was not completed for troop trials as Prototype 138 until 1926. It served with the 16ème Escadron d'Automitrailleuses, but it was found to perform poorly off road with only one driven axle, and had a high ground pressure due to its narrow tyres. A revival of the old Genty specification was then attempted in the 1922–26 period on the basis of a 16hp chassis, but the value of an unarmoured body was by then only of passing interest to the army. The experience underlined the need for specialist chassis design and highlighted several areas where Panhard could improve. The mistake was not repeated.

The failure of Prototype 138 really fired Panhard's designers (and management board) into making far more serious effort at interesting the army in a fully armoured, turreted armoured car. The Panhard Auto Mitrailleuse de Découverte 165 (or AMD 165) had a longer and slightly narrower wheelbase than the Prototype 138 chassis with a well-designed armoured body that made maximum use of angled plates to deflect bullets. Vision from the vehicle (critical for all crew members) was more carefully studied during the design phase, incorporating a larger number of small shuttered vision ports. Motive power was provided by an 80hp, 4.85-litre 4-cylinder ISK 4 F8 engine without sleeve valves, a type already in extensive use in Panhard cars and trucks.

The AMD 165 entered production in 1929 and it was followed by the almost identical AMD 175 in 1932. Both types were adopted (without much distinction between the two models) by the French Army. The first 28 AMD 165s were sent directly to Morocco to serve in two 14-car squadrons (3 platoons of 4 cars with 2 spares held in a platoon headquarters section). The later cars with 86hp engines were known as AMD 175 TOE (TOE was an abbreviation for Territoires d'Opérations Extérieurs), easily distinguished by lateral radiator condensers, additional to the one mounted on the front of the engine compartment. These were vehicles built for counter-insurgency in the harsh terrain of North Africa and the Middle East and were well regarded in service.

The AMD 175 TOE was an impressive vehicle for its time – a 6.7-tonne vehicle with a road speed of 60kmh, a 37mm Mle 1918 main armament and a 7.5mm machine-gun with a crew of 4 men. At least 50 were built, and the type served in Syria, Morocco and Algeria (in some cases through the Second World War and into its aftermath). A second personnel carrier/cargo variant on the same chassis was equipped with a large armoured box body and armed with a single machine-gun. Its body included side gun ports permitting its passengers to defend themselves in case of ambush. The AMD 165 and AMD 175 were by no means as successful as Panhard would have liked, there having been less than 100 of both types built, but the 1930s were lean years for the colonial army.

The AMD 178

Panhard's designers returned to the drawing board with the goal of designing a much more specialised vehicle, in hopes of selling the army a standard armoured car for use in Europe. The resulting design was certainly one of the world's best armoured cars when the Second World War broke out in 1939.

The Panhard AMD 178 was designed under the supervision of Louis Delagarde, a young engineer who knew armoured vehicles. He had served in the Artillerie Spéciale as a Renault FT commander in 1918, and his brother had served in St Chamond tanks. The first prototype AMD was under construction in 1933 and in 1934 the prototype (less turret, which was the APX 3 on production vehicles, designed by the Atelier de Construction de Puteaux, although a small provisional turret was fitted for trial), was under test at Vincennes.

The AMD 178 chassis was designed to run with power to the rear wheels on roads and with power to all wheels in cross-country mode. The hull armour plates were riveted and were inclined wherever possible to deflect bullets. The AMD 178 employed a rear-engined

layout and included a rear driver's position, although the latter could only be employed with the transmission in all-wheel drive mode and visibility was limited. The prototype could ascend a 50% grade and could easily reach 70kmh on paved roads. The army was impressed and adopted the type as the 'AMD Panhard Mle 1935', and production began in 1935. The APX 3 turret mounted a 25mm anti-tank cannon and a 7.5mm machine-gun with 150 and 3,750 rounds of ammunition respectively, its 145 litres of fuel permitted a range of 300km on roads, and it was served by a crew of four men. A command version with a fixed wireless casemate instead of a turret was provided for each squadron. These cars, like many French AFVs of 1939–40, would certainly have given a more memorable performance in battle had they been provided with wireless sets, especially in the reconnaissance role. Plans existed to improve the AMD 178 into a larger family of vehicles but these were never realised as events unfolded in 1940.

By 1939, some 360 AMD 35s were in service, and in 1940 the type proved effective in combat, superior to all German armoured cars and even effective against the lighter variants

ABOVE This AMD 35 Panhard 178 is from the first production batch that was delivered from February 1937. It displays the characteristic camouflage scheme of the immediate pre-war period incorporating green and grey colours outlined in black. The vehicle featured two-wheel drive on roads and all four in cross-country mode. The AMD 178 employed a rear-engine layout and included a rear driver's position for rapid withdrawal in reverse gear.

ABOVE Although a wide range of variants of the AMD 35 was proposed, few were produced beyond the Voiture Blindée Poste de Commande pour ER 27 as seen here abandoned in Belgium on 20 May 1940 with a standard AMD 35 in the background. Lacking the usual 25mm cannon, the AMD radio command vehicle featured radio masts at front and rear and 24 were built in 1939. *(Getty Images)*

of the Panzers they faced. After the French surrender, the Germans transferred 64 AMD 35s to the Vichy Armée de l'Armistice with 25mm guns removed, with 28 others held in reserve.

Most of the damaged AMD 35s recuperated from the battles of 1940 were returned by the Germans to the Panhard factory to be cannibalised or rebuilt. Another 45 AMDs, unfinished at the time of the armistice, were hidden in southern France prior to the occupation of Paris. Of all the captured armoured cars and AFVs produced by France to be taken into Wehrmacht service, the AMD 35 was by far the most admired. As the Panzerwagen P 204 (f) Type 178 the type was widely used. Possibly over 200 examples were employed by both the Wehrmacht and the Waffen SS, some serving right up to 1945 on nearly all fronts. As these were damaged or used to the point of requiring rebuilding, they were returned to the care of the Panhard factory where Paul and Jean Panhard headed repair efforts.

Panhard's 'collaboration' concealed long-term efforts by the firm to supply armoured car bodies and suitable chassis to resistance elements – armée secrète – at extremely high risk. In the second half of 1944, these secret armoured cars were employed against the Germans along the Atlantic seaboard. The AMD 178s recaptured from the Germans continued in service after the liberation, and the AMD 178 was put back into full production as the AMD

178 B, with a new Fives-Lille F1 cast turret armed with a 47mm gun and a Reibel 7.5mm gun, armoured to 15mm standard all around. The army had been waiting for this second large AMD order since 1942, when General De Metz had stated the need to an unwilling Vichy general staff.

The post-war era: from AMD 178B to EBR

Panhard's production line had been maintained intact throughout the war and in all 200 AMD 178B were built for the returning FFL (Free French Forces) Army, the first few participating in the 14 July parade of 1945. It is worthy of note that hardly any other French AFV manufacturer could successfully manufacture a complete armoured vehicle in 1944–46; one has only to look at the farcical result of the ARL44 programme conducted at the same time.

The AMD 178B differed in more than just its turret from the prewar model. It employed a new 110hp engine without sleeve valves, the 4 HL type designed in 1940 and intended to be used commercially in Panhard lorries. The new engine would continue in production throughout the 1950s. The AMD 178B was used in combat in Indochina, in North Africa and in the Levant, some having been gifted to the Syrian Army once the French quelled the rising in Damascus in 1954. In Djibouti the type continued in use until 1960.

Panhard had started work on a more advanced eight-wheeled armoured car known as the Auto Mitrailleuse de Reconnaissance 201 (or AMR 201) to supplement or replace the AMD 178 before the Second World War erupted. The first prototype featured a transversely mounted six-cylinder without sleeve valves displacing 3.834 litres for an output of 85hp. The central pairs of wheels were arranged to be lowered or raised hydraulically, used only for crossing poor terrain. These wheels were all-metal with lugged treads for maximum traction. The transmission gave 16 speeds in forward and as many in reverse, with drivers' positions both fore and aft. (A range of these speeds employed all eight wheels while others, intended strictly for paved roads, employed the front and rear pairs of driven wheels alone with the central ones raised.)

This advanced (and complex) project was supported by the war minister Raoul Dautry and was presented to General Gamelin just before the outbreak of war. Dautry told Jean Panhard that he intended to order 600 of these vehicles as soon as trials were completed, turreted armament of a 25mm anti-tank gun and 7.5mm machine-gun being envisioned for the short term, with a more powerful armament under consideration. Once war broke out, priority changed to getting as many AMD 35s as possible completed for the

BELOW In the immediate post-war period, it took some time to reconstruct French industry including armament manufacturers. Accordingly, French armed forces continued to rely on American equipment for several years. An exception was the Panhard 178 armoured car that resumed production in July 1945 but with a new FL1 turret mounting a 47mm SA35 cannon, as shown here. Such vehicles were readily deployed to French Indochina to reclaim the former colonies lost to the Japanese. Designated the Panhard 178B, the vehicle was popular with its crews and was known affectionately as 'Pan Pan'.

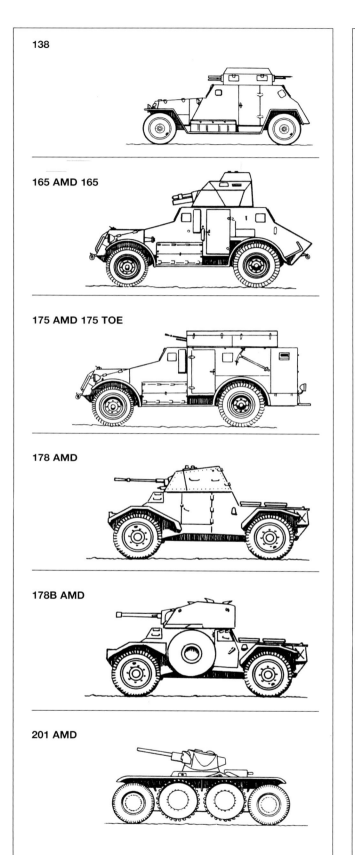

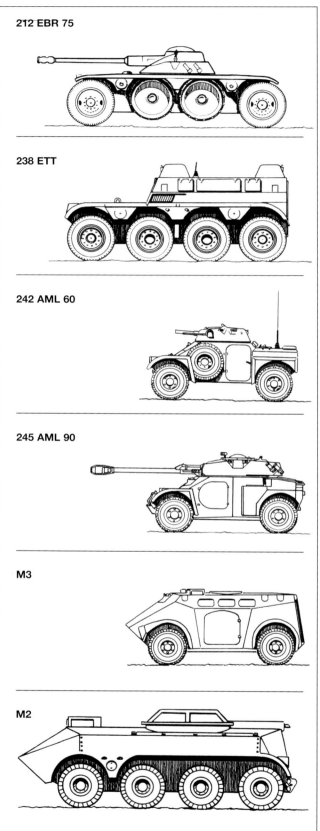

138

165 AMD 165

175 AMD 175 TOE

178 AMD

178B AMD

201 AMD

212 EBR 75

238 ETT

242 AML 60

245 AML 90

M3

M2

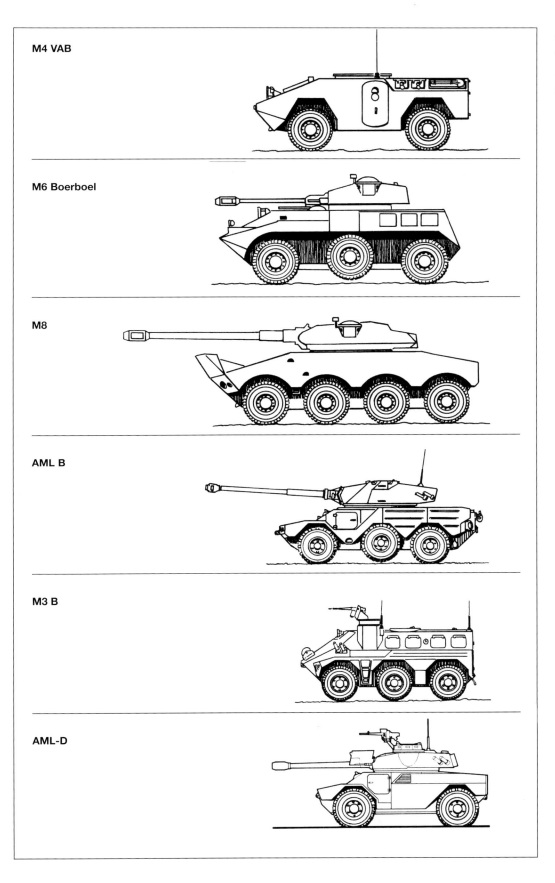

M4 VAB

M6 Boerboel

M8

AML B

M3 B

AML-D

THIS SPREAD
Timeline of the
Panhard family of
armoured cars.

ABOVE The M8 and M20 range of armoured cars was still the mainstay of the French cavalry units during the Indochina and Algerian conflicts. This M8 from the 18ème Régiment de Dragons is seen in the Medjerda valley in north-eastern Algeria protecting farmers at harvest time. Note the non-standard but regularly employed .50 ring mount on the turret as fitted to the M20 Armoured Utility Car. As veterans of the Second World War, these vehicles were not only ill-suited to the Algerian terrain and type of warfare since most were worn out, but they were also hampered by a lack of spare parts.

BELOW A pair of EBRs demonstrates their considerable cross-country agility with their centre wheels lowered for increased traction. These vehicles have the FL10 turret with the lengthened 75mm guns that were liable to spiking in the ground, as seen on the rear EBR, and difficult to manoeuvre in wooded terrain. It was, however, a powerful armoured car and well suited to its role of reconnaissance in the European theatre of operations.

French Army. In the disaster of 1940 the AMR 201 prototype was embarked on a cargo ship bound for North Africa to prevent it falling into German hands (although the latter were not yet aware of its existence). Its fate was thereafter lost to history – some record it was part of the cargo of the merchant ship *Massilia*, sunk en route, others record it was immured in a quarry near Rabat and forgotten to history, and others that it was scrapped in 1952.

In 1945 the FFL army of General de Gaulle stated a requirement to replace the M8, an American armoured car in widespread use and generously provided under Lend Lease. The M8 did not fill the army's future needs, being poorly armed by 1945 standards, as well as being thinly armoured. In 1945 the AMR 201 project was revisited with Panhard by IGA Etienne Roland, then chief of the newly established DEFA's research bureau. The concept of front and rear driving positions was considered excellent in a reconnaissance vehicle, and the chassis was large enough to accept a large and powerfully armed turret. The engine would have to be mounted in the centre of the chassis underneath the turret, and needed to be as low in profile as possible (and of flat layout). Panhard had already built such an engine (in 2-cylinder form) for the Dyna, and a 12-cylinder flat engine was designed for this new heavy armoured car. Through 1948, Panhard engineers Delagarde and Gery put their full-time efforts into the design of the new air-cooled engine, the one old Panhard hand tempering the ideas of the other in the practical in turn. This was typical of how the company's design teams worked, in an intimate environment where loyalty to the firm and the feeling of family pervaded. The design they came up with was original and promising.

Hydraulics would by necessity be of extreme importance in such an ambitious design with retractable wheels. The crankshaft and crankcase were both innovative designs, torsion bars were developed for the suspension. The finished design weighed 13 tonnes and could manage a roadspeed of 115kmh. Off-road the new Panhard could climb a 60% gradient, cross a 2m trench and ford a 1.2m-deep stream. Fives-Lille, the design bureau that had designed the 47mm turret for the AMD 178B, designed an oscillating turret for the eight-wheel chassis.

Armed with a 75mm CN 75 Mle 49 gun and a co-axial MAC-31 machine-gun in an oscillating FL11 two-man turret, the Engin Blindé de Reconnaissance Panhard (or EBR) packed the same punch as an M4 Sherman tank. The CN-75-49 fired compatible ammunition to the US M3 75mm gun, itself a development of the French Mle 97 'Soixante-Quinze'. This vehicle was, to the untrained eye, a wheeled tank.

The EBR was large enough to carry a crew of four along with 56 rounds of 75mm ammunition and 2,200 rounds of 7.5mm ammunition for its three machine-guns. The complexity of the design presented many challenges in the development of the starter, the electrical and especially the hydraulic systems that took much effort at the Avenue d'Ivry plant to resolve. Ultimately the EBR 75 was successfully adopted in 1951 and was further developed through the 1950s into the most powerful armoured car of its type anywhere.

After unit tests alongside the AMX 13 in 1952, the EBR entered service in Algeria and elsewhere in North Africa with French cavalry units. The Panhard EBR was well regarded as an effective combat vehicle in both the patrol, convoy escort and reconnaissance roles in Algeria. The EBR was as good a gun platform as any armoured car of its era could have been. It was stable firing fore and aft and rocked noticeably when firing in the 3 and 9 o'clock positions, especially in the case of the cars equipped with the FL10 turret. EBR's required well-trained drivers and, whatever the complexity of the EBR's mechanicals most

ABOVE AND BELOW From 1956, the Panhard EBR began to supersede the wartime M8 Greyhound armoured car within the 1er Régiment Étranger Cavalerie. The EBR was technically more complex than its predecessor so to test the equipment fully it was decided to mount an expedition under the harshest conditions in the Algerian desert. Beginning on 6 January 1958, the mission was to cover some 4,000 miles comprising a caravan of six EBRs supported by Hotchkiss M201 Jeeps as well as five Berliet 10T and 16 Dodge 6 x 6 trucks of the 2nd Saharan Transport Company. Three of the EBRs travelled with the original steel central wheels and three with low-pressure X4 Michelin tyres in their place. Under the command of Major Dorot, the vehicles travelled from Constantine via Biskra to the desert around Ouragla and on to Tamanrasset near the Niger border by 5 February. The convoy returned to Constantine on 15 February having validated the EBR as suitable for service with the Foreign Legion.

problems arose with badly treated clutches and transmissions due to rushed driver training. The EBR was surprisingly manoeuvrable, performing turns on a highway at speed with little risk of rolling over. French cavalry armoured car units could rely completely on the EBR for offensive needs and with the EBR they packed a punch that was unparalleled in the reconnaissance units of many allied armies.

Hydraulic failures were the most common problem with the design in service, the rupture of a flexible hydraulic line inevitably coating the driver or gunner with oil and was followed by the central pairs of steel wheels (called roues agricoles or 'tractor wheels' by the crews and even at Panhard) slowly descending into ground contact. These broken lines could be easily fixed by the crew but were a source of enragement or amusement depending on what position you sat in. Its extractor fans were woefully inadequate and, after firing the main armament for any length of time the hatches had to be opened lest the crew faint for powder fumes and the heat from firing.

A notable step in the progression of the EBR design was the evaluation of the EBR chassis to fit the AMX 13's FL10 turret armed with the CN-75-50, a high-velocity anti-tank gun with a range of 1,000m and quite capable of knocking out any medium tank of the 1950s (and many still a decade later). This modification added about a ton of weight to the design, but the chassis and suspension were more than up to it.

EBRs were vulnerable like any lightly armoured vehicle to enemy artillery, infantry

BELOW The Engin Blindé de Reconnaissance (EBR) was produced in two major versions from 1950 to 1960. The original model, as seen on the left, featured an FL11 turret mounting a 75mm gun derived from that of the German Panther tank, and capable of firing AP rounds with a muzzle velocity of 1,970ft/sec. The second model, to the right, incorporated an FL10 turret of the AMX 13 light tank with a lengthened 75mm gun with a muzzle velocity of 3,280ft/sec but at the expense of height and weight. In 1963, both weapons were superseded by the 90mm D921/F1 smooth-bore gun as fitted to the AML Type 245/AML 90. This weapon was mounted in the FL11 turret to return the EBR to its original dimensions but now with a weapon of superior armour-piercing capability.

RIGHT The French Army employed both the Ferret Mk 1 and Mk 2 in Algeria with 200 procured from Britain during the conflict. This Ferret Mk 2 belongs to the 1er Régiment de Chasseurs d'Afrique, as denoted by the regimental insignia on the rear hull plate. It was one of the premier units to use the Ferret during the Algerian campaign. Originally designed to the British concept of reconnaissance by stealth, the Ferret lacked the firepower to be truly effective in the hilly terrain of Algeria and armed with just a single machine-gun it was unable to engage the fedayeen hidden in the high ground. Furthermore, the open-topped Mk 1 was vulnerable to attack from above. Accordingly, the requirement for the AML demanded both heavier armament and a fully enclosed two-man turret.

anti-tank weapons and mines, and in Algeria a number were lost in combat. Many of the EBRs serving in the 1950s in Algeria covered huge mileages, 10,000km being not unheard of. On a good road the EBR could easily outrun a Jeep, and it was a commercial success for Panhard with over 1200 being ordered for the French Army (armed with the FL11 turret or with the high-velocity gunned, auto-loaded FL10 turret shared with the AMX 13). After 1964 the FL11-turreted vehicles were upgraded with more powerful guns and the type served until the early 1980s. The type had the confidence of its crews throughout a long service life.

A small export order for the EBR was placed by Portugal in 1956. This consisted of 50 of the EBR FL10s and 28 ETT (Engin Transport de Troupes armoured personnel carriers), produced by designing an APC body to be employed on an EBR chassis instead of a turreted fighting compartment. The ETT was only purchased by Portugal and could carry a crew of two (driver and commander) as well as 12 fully equipped troops in the rear. Smaller orders for EBRs were placed by West Germany for evaluation (they were later employed by the Federal Border Police) and also by Indonesia.

Panhard was not focused on exports at the time the EBR was being produced, and it counted its success in the 1950s on building and rebuilding the French cavalry's impressive EBR fleet as a major commercial focus. This came to change in the following decade.

BELOW In order to increase the firepower of the Ferret armoured car during the Algerian War, the vehicle was fitted with the M20 75mm recoilless rifle that was an effective weapon against ground targets such as sangars but it did expose the operator to an unacceptable degree. Trials were also conducted with the Ferret Mk 1 but only the Ferret Mk 2 with M20 saw action in Algeria.

The AML

The EBR programme was pursued while the French Army general staff conducted a separate programme to procure a light armoured car for the future. Colonial wars continued throughout the entire decade of the 1950s and brought the armoured car into a more important position as a major weapon in the French cavalry's armoury. Armoured cars were recognised as a vital weapon for counter-insurgency, and had already played an important part in the long war in Indochina. The campaign in Algeria was proving a difficult and bloody series of operations where the armoured car again proved its usefulness. The

M8 Greyhound, Daimler Ferret and Panhard EBR had all served with varying degrees of success in Algeria, but none of these vehicles was ideal for the kind of warfare the French Army had to fight in the rugged terrain of Algeria. The Greyhound was old, spares were growing scarce, and it was armed with a 37mm weapon that fired but a small high explosive round and was useless against modern AFVs. The Ferret was a nimble scout car, but for all of its versatility it utterly lacked any weapon more powerful than a .30-calibre machine-gun. Its two-man crew was also considered inadequate for French preferences. The EBR was a brilliant and heavily armed weapon, ideal for reconnaissance work in Europe. It really proved out of its element in the steep hill country of Algeria, a war it had never been designed for. It was heavy, maintenance intensive, road bound by the very complexity of its mechanicals and especially vulnerable to mines.

What the army needed was an armoured car

LEFT Illustrious members of the Panhard team pose besides a Type 242 model prototype undergoing running trials at Ermenonville. The vehicle shows the driver's foul weather cover as fitted to the EBR. At left in the beret is M. Roger Cotinot, official Panhard test-driver. He joined the Panhard Company in 1928 at the age of 14 and left in 1976 as head of the prototype testing department.

that combined the best attributes of these three armoured vehicles to create an ideal AFV for counter-insurgency work. If such a vehicle could be produced quickly it might be able to make a lasting impact on the bloody conflict raging in the Maghreb. The worsening situation in Algeria had already spurred the EMA to demand development of a light armoured car (Auto Mitrailleuse Légère or AML) designs in February 1955. One possibility was to buy more British Ferrets (or even to build them under licence), and the second was to produce a French design of similar size. The AML requirement was defined in terms of tonnage (4.2 tonnes), range of 500km and basic armament (originally two MGs and a 'grenade launcher') on 19 March 1956. The vehicle had to be air-portable, capable of fording 0.8m streams, as well as having an amphibious capability, with a crew of three. Some 2,000 vehicles were expected to be required for French needs, by both the air force as airfield defence vehicles and by the army. This vehicle was expected to weigh a third as much as an EBR and to be no larger than the Ferret.

Despite the obvious need, the AML project received a low priority from the army until 1958. The army's budget was split by then between war in Algeria and increasing France's NATO commitment with conventional armoured and infantry divisions for the defence of West Germany. The quickest solution was complicated by the refusal of Panhard and Berliet to licence-produce the Ferret.

Over 200 Ferrets had already been bought to replace the M8 Greyhound, which the French could only maintain in dwindling numbers as spares became scarce. The Ferrets bought from the British included both Mk 1s and Mk 2s. The Mk 1s employed by the French Army occasionally mounted weapons as heavy as the 75mm recoilless rifle, which was symptomatic of the Ferret's biggest disadvantage: a weak armament.

The AML programme was certainly attractive to several French manufacturers and included a notable number of private automakers in an arms market which was increasingly dominated by DEFA or nationalised manufacturers. Renault was keen on producing an AML, while Simca (Société

Industrielle de Mécanique et Carrosserie Automobile) was willing only to produce these as part of a larger production group. Drawings for AML proposals were finalised from Berliet, AMX, Saviem and Panhard. Saviem and Panhard moved quickly to produce prototypes during 1957. Both were endorsed by DEFA for further consideration, while DEFA's own AMX-designed AML prototype proceeded into development with a lower priority (as a failsafe). The Saviem (Société Anonyme de Véhicules Industriels et d'Equipements Mécaniques, a Renault subsidiary) vehicle could mount a Simca or Renault engine. The Saviem design had a large hull without side doors, partly because it was intended to have an amphibious capacity.

Panhard began its initial AML project with the design concept of an armoured car with two men in the hull and a single man in the turret. The light armoured car specification was sufficiently demanding that the engineers in Panhard's Avenue d'Ivry (including Delagarde) started from scratch in a bid to secure this new venture for Panhard. The light armoured car had to be everything the EBR was not: light, simpler in concept and cheap. Only the EBR's helical spring suspension and drive shaft system were carried forward into the new design, known as Prototype 242, which was started in 1957. The Arme Blindée Cavalerie had already enough experience of armoured car operations in Indochina to demand a two-man turret, and so DEFA stepped in. St Chamond was assigned the task of designing an adequate turret, which was shown in wooden model form to Panhard in July 1956.

By late 1957 it was decided not to series produce the Saviem AML unless the Panhard model failed, but like the AMX proposal the development of the Saviem hull was completed. The Saviem and Panhard AML hull prototypes were ready for evaluation as wooden models and subsequently in steel between June 1957 and early 1958. Both prototypes were tested out with the FL13 turret designed by Fives-Lille. It was armed with a 60mm mortar and two machine-guns. The first of three Fives-Lille FL13 turrets was delivered in normal steel in October

1957; two more were delivered in 1958. DEFA's intention to arm the AML with its own turret was also accepted but this took another year to see the light of day.

The definitive AML prototype was completed in mild steel by Panhard in 1959, designated Panhard AML 242. The rear of the AML's hull evolved considerably between Prototype 242's construction and that of the production vehicles. The 4-HD petrol engine that Panhard offered for the AML 242 in particular was new, but it followed Panhard's design practices. It used the Panhard Dyna engine's cylinders and valves with an original flat-4 layout. Each cylinder had an individual camshaft and each cylinder had a 500cu cm displacement, giving the 90hp (4,300 rpm) engine a diminutive 2-litre displacement.

The four-wheeled hull showed typical Panhard design characteristics, and if viewed from the front it showed a clear EBR lineage. The angled front plate arrangement had been adopted for the EBR's hull front due to the experience of repairing battle-damaged AMD 178 hulls, which were predominantly victims of penetration of the hull front. The EBR's armour configuration had been proven in Algeria and was carried forward to the AML hull design. The engine was mounted in the hull rear and cardan shafts, supplied power to the wheels, running along the hull edges in a broadly lozenge-shaped arrangement.

Prototype 242 tested through 1959 still employed the low-profile Panhard turret with a central mortar mounting with two lateral machine-gun mountings. Large stowage bins encased the rear wheels. The French Army rejected the FL13 turret design, but the hull was accepted for production as the Panhard Type 245. The armoured car was adopted with four general mission types in mind: 1. line of communication security; 2. security of vulnerable locales; 3. reconnaissance missions; and 4. air transportable, quick deployable intervention missions.

The AML's turret underwent its own evolution after the FL13 was rejected so the AML's turret design responsibility was passed from St Chamond to the Atelier du Havre (AHE) at the same time that the Panhard hull design was finalised while AHE finished the development of the HB 60mm 'lance grenade' breech-loading mortar and twin 7.5mm machine-gun armed turret. The AHE turret was conical in shape, featuring a single roof hatch and a twin-mantlet weapons mounting in the centreline of the turret face, with the ability to elevate the machine guns separately from the mortar or to link them in order to function as a true co-axial weapons mount. The 60mm breech-loading mortar was adopted after testing the German 20mm

MG151 and the US M2 12.5mm Browning. The adoption of this turret on the Panhard hull was ultimately the form taken by the Panhard AML 245 we know today as the AML HE 60. It was ordered in two forms, both armed with the 60mm Mortier CS as the primary weapon and with either twin AA 52 7.5mm MGs or with a single 12.7mm Browning-type HMG.

The AHE also designed a 90mm gunned turret, with the dual purpose of a possible

ABOVE Another prototype of the DEFA-AMX model deleted the side doors to provide an amphibious capability. The AHE (Atelier du Havre) turret seen here was eventually preferred to the Panhard proposal and finally selected for production. This turret incorporates a .50cal HB Browning in place of the two 7.5mm AA-52 machine-guns and became a production variant in its own right as AML 60-12, the 12 indicating the weapon calibre in millimetres as in 12.7mm.

LEFT The original turret mounting the 90mm F1 gun was produced by AHE that evolved into the definitive AML 90 model. Here the turret is shown on the chassis of the DEFA-AMX d'AML SL 420.

stability even at the 3 o'clock and 9 o'clock positions. The AML H90 turret was now so powerfully armed that no foreign armoured car design of comparable size and weight could remotely compete. Here was a vehicle no heavier than a Ferret, but capable of destroying an enemy medium tank.

The AML had only four wheels and a relatively small wheel base, but it handled very well off-road, crossing a .8m trench, and climbing a 60% gradient. The gearbox design was critical in permitting this cross-country performance, with three speeds designed for off-road and four speeds designed for use on roads. The hull floor plate was perfectly smooth to prevent snagging but its interior profile was V-shaped to maximise mine resistance. The patented Panhard gearbox also prevented any single wheel spinning to the detriment of traction on the other three stations, in fact the system transferred any reserve of power to the wheel exerting the best tractive effort. On soft, sandy ground the crew could lower tyre pressure, and the pressure could be increased with the AML's on-board compressor. Each tyre incorporated an inflatable Hutchinson inner tube section with an inner core with multiple gas filled compartments. These tyres were certainly not intended to be bullet proof, but rather puncture-resistant.

A ten-vehicle pre-production series of AMLs was produced by Panhard in early 1959 as DEFA wanted to avoid buying any more Ferrets. Meanwhile, the Saviem AML project

ABOVE The AHE designed a 90mm gun turret as a possible armament for a wheeled version of the Engin Léger de Combat that was first mounted on the experimental (DEFA) AMX AML SL420 hull and then that of the Panhard 245. This turret was ordered for the AML 90 after testing on the third mild steel prototype built by Panhard and on the AMX AML S420. The low-pressure CN-90-F1 fired a powerful fin-stabilised HEAT round at relatively modest velocity and the gun was perfected in 1959.

RIGHT When Saviem withdrew from the AML competition, development of the DEFA-AMX carried on in case the Panhard version failed. When the latter was chosen for production, testing of the 90mm turret mounted on the AMX hull continued.

armament for a wheeled version of the ELC (Engin Léger de Combat) which was first mounted on the experimental (DEFA) AMX AML SL420 hull and then that of the Panhard 245. This turret was ordered for the AML 90 after testing on the third mild steel prototype built by Panhard and on the AMX AML S420. The low-pressure CN-90-F1 fired a powerful fin-stabilised HEAT round at relatively modest velocity and the gun was perfected in 1959.

The HE 60 and HE 90 turrets were subcontracted for manufacture by the Compagnie Normande de Mécanique de Précision. The DEFA 90mm gun could be fired at any point of traverse, the AML H90's 5,500kg rocking forcefully but maintaining

ABOVE The combination of the AHE turret with its powerful 90mm F1 gun and the compact hull of the Panhard Type 245 first underwent trials in 1961. Minor modifications were made to the hull to accommodate the larger turret, most noticeable being the rear bins that were sloped downwards on production vehicles to allow greater depression of the gun when facing rearwards, and such items as the gun crutch were deleted.

RIGHT One of the ten pre-production vehicles shows the marriage of the AHE 60 turret with the hull of the Panhard Type 245 hull. The latter now features the spare wheel on the side door but retains the straight-side rear bins and air intake.

was dropped. The DEFA AMX AML S420 was not dropped for another year and was still in consideration in the event of the Panhard programme encountering problems. The first Panhard AML 60s were delivered to the army in April and May 1959. At the same time the design of an amphibious APC employing the same chassis was requested from Panhard by DEFA.

RIGHT A late AML 90 prototype is put through its paces during trials in 1962. It is now fitted with an un-ditching channel across the front that became so characteristic of the AML series as well as Michelin XL run-flat tyres.

Chapter Two

The AML in French service

While the eight-wheel EBR was well suited for operations in Europe, the Panhard AML proved highly effective across the world, particularly in Africa with the French Rapid Intervention Forces that were employed wherever French interests were threatened or endangered. The arrival of a squadron of AMLs together with French Foreign Legionnaires was often enough to quell civil unrest across francophone Africa.

OPPOSITE French paratroopers of 2ème Régiment Étranger de Parachutists patrol the streets of Beirut as part of the Multinational Force in Lebanon on 23 August 1982, supported by AML 90s of the Régiment d'Infanterie-Chars de Marine. (Getty Images)

35

The beginning of the 1960s was a period of extensive reform in the French Army. The changing concept of how land forces were to be employed was felt right down to the squadron and platoon level in the Arme Blindée Cavalerie. The threat of the Warsaw Pact's vast forces brought about a change of doctrine in how the army intended to defend the French interior that was deemed vulnerable to infiltration by Special Forces, sabotage and paratroop drops. The Défense Opérationnelle du Territoire (or DOT) doctrine, a 1962 revision to a general principle first tabled in 1959, saw the army's light wheeled armoured units (especially Chasseur regiments) earmarked to respond to enemy actions on French territory.

AML units proved ideal for this role, while units equipped with the older EBR (in the main Hussard regiments) were still well suited to serve as reconnaissance units for the Corps de Bataille stationed in West Germany. Armoured

The first AMLs were successfully tested in the field in Algeria by the 12ème Régiment de Dragons at the end of 1961 as the bitter conflict came to an end. One of the results was that the AML programme so vital to the counter-insurgency campaign decreased in priority as the army turned its efforts almost exclusively towards France's NATO commitments (and towards acquiring a nuclear capability independent of its allies). The French Army's AML order was cut from 2,000 vehicles to a mere 600 of all types.

RIGHT The combination of an AML 60 and 90 is the basis of a scout platoon, offering a wide range of tactical options for the commander depending on the nature of the threat. Differing from the British doctrine, reconnaissance missions in France may rely on opening fire on an identified enemy in order to evaluate his reactions, thus providing information about his future intentions. The AML 60-12 in the foreground mounts a coaxial 12.7mm HB Browning in place of the usual twin 7.62m machine-guns.

and mechanised units equipped with the M47 and AMX 13, meanwhile, were earmarked to serve as the main armoured force in the Forces Françaises en Allemagne. The potential enemy would be commando forces infiltrated into the country from its coasts or through parachute landings. Communications, strategic industries and base areas were all vulnerable in these scenarios and wheeled armour proved an excellent means of quick response. Soviet airborne forces in particular were known to deploy air-landed or parachutable armoured vehicles such as the ASU 57 and ASU 85. In a secondary function, AML units could equally be used to engage enemy reconnaissance units equipped with vehicles like the BRDM, BMP, BMD or PT 76. In a last recourse, AML units could be used to attack enemy lines of communications, logistics and support services.

The end of the Algerian War saw the French Army general staff's AML order reduced from 2,000 to 600 vehicles, in multiple small batches. In the end some 784 vehicles were ordered for the French Army, including 512 AML 60s, 260 AML 90s, and 12 AML D90 Lynx (fitted with a diesel engine for the 4ème Régiment de Chasseurs at Gap). The Gendarmerie Nationale ordered a further 121 AMLs (73 AML 60 CS with the special 60mm mortar and 48 AML H90 F1).

The total number speaks for how well the AML fits into the French Army's doctrine for overseas deployment (particularly in former colonial areas), its new doctrine for territorial defence and for the AML's general qualities as a combat vehicle – where it became justly famous for its simplicity, its firepower and its low cost to buy and operate. These were all characteristics that attracted a great deal of interest from foreign clientele, which transformed the global market for wheeled light reconnaissance vehicles.

ABOVE An AML 60-12 belonging to the 5ème Régiment de Chasseurs is seen during an exercise in wooded terrain during the mid-1970s. The use of mud as an improvised camouflage scheme was common practice among crews at this time. This is a definitive model of this version with Michelin XL tyres and twin spotlights on the turret.

LEFT An AML platoon belonging to the Groupement Blindé de la Gendarmerie Nationale (GBGN) stands on parade at their base in Satory to the west of Paris. A total of 121 AMLs saw service with the Gendarmerie within the GBGN and were employed on internal security duties.

RIGHT With red material wrapped around the barrel of the 90mm gun to indicate enemy forces, an AML 90 takes part in a military exercise. Both the 90 and the 60 were very cramped inside – the 90 especially – so much personal kit had to be carried on the outside of the vehicles when on exercise or operations as ammunition must take priority.

Export success

The AML's promise and the disappointment of the reduction in the French order pushed Panhard towards marketing the AML in allied countries and in the developing world. The degree to which Panhard successfully pursued this surprised many at the time, a period when American arms were being marketed with tremendous success in the western world. Panhard immediately began to orient the AML towards the export market. René Panhard –

son of Hyppolite Panhard and grandson of the pioneer René Panhard – had worked in the family firm since the late 1920s and had spent the war as one of France's best fighter pilots. He was an instrumental figure in Panhard's efforts to export the AML.

The export armoured car market was dominated in the 1950s and early 1960s by the Daimler Ferret and Alvis Saladin families from Britain. Besides the small EBR order for Portugal, the export market was one that Panhard (and by extension France) had long failed to penetrate and had never prioritised. The arrival of the AML changed the landscape of the market entirely, by nature of its heavy armament and its design with a crew of three.

In the developing world the AML proved an ideal and affordable weapon suited equally well to defence or internal security missions. Panhard developed many variations on the basic AML and M3 platforms to suit customer

LEFT The Ferret Mk 2 was armed with a single 7.62mm machine-gun and weighed 3.7 tons. The AML 90 had a 90mm gun and coaxial 7.5mm machine-gun while weighing 5.5 tonnes. The difference in firepower is marked with the DEFA 921 F1 gun capable of defeating 320mm of armour out to 1,500m. With a height of just 6ft 9in (2.07m), the AML is compact and is well suited to reconnaissance by stealth but with more than sufficient firepower to fight its way out of trouble.

needs. In time the AML eclipsed the light Ferret and the heavier Saladin, for it was either more heavily armed or lighter than either, and was less expensive than the latter. The AML 90's 90mm OCC-62 DEFA hollow charge round had an anti-tank performance in excess of that offered on any other 5- to 6-ton wheeled vehicle, and could also fire high-explosive and smoke rounds out to 1,000m accurately.

The AML 60 could also be fitted with an ENTAC missile launching system for long-range anti-tank defence, fulfilling a role similar to the

ABOVE One of the fundamental design requirements for the AML was its ability to be transported to any area where French interests may be threatened. The Transall C-160 seen here can carry up to two AMLs while the C-130 Hercules has a cargo capacity of three. However, especially under African climatic conditions, the load capacity and operating range of such transport aircraft can be significantly reduced when flying in hot air temperatures.

contemporary Ferret Vigilant. The SAMO 1160 launcher carried four ENTACs stowed behind the turret, with pairs of missiles on rails on each side of the turret when folded outward

LEFT The AML 60 could also be fitted with an ENTAC missile launching system for long-range anti-tank defence, fulfilling a role similar to the contemporary Ferret Vigilant. The SAMO 1160 launcher carried four ENTACs stowed behind the turret, with pairs of missiles on rails on each side of the turret when folded outward ready to launch. The AML 90 was in time offered with SS-11 missile launching capability as well.

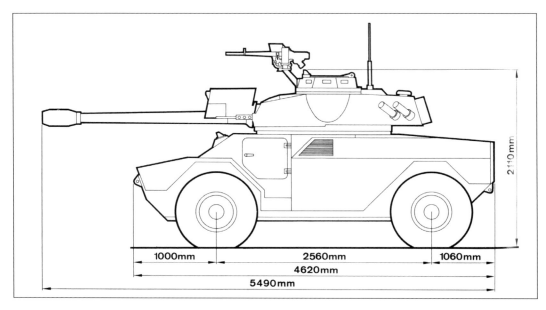

1000mm 2560mm 1060mm
4620mm
5490mm

2110mm

ready to launch. The AML 90 was in time offered with SS11 missile launching capability as well, although it is not known that any were successfully marketed.

In all, 36 countries went on to order AML H60s, AML H90s and the M3 armoured personnel carrier derived directly from the AML chassis. The AML's 4-HD engine was also proposed to equip the series production Marmon-Bocquet 4 x 4 light tactical truck, although it was in the end built with a Ford sleeve-valve V8 engine. Many years later in 1978, the AML-D (with many ELC features) was proposed by Panhard as a turbo diesel-engined AML version, equipped with a 3-litre, 115hp (4,200rpm) 5-cylinder Mercedes-Benz OM-617A engine.

The AML in French Army service

Europe and Africa

AMLs were operated in specialised armoured car regiments in the French Army, known by the term Régiment de Cavalerie Légère Blindée (CLB) des Forces du Territoire. In the Arme Blindée Cavalerie the AML and EBR units were known as 'la légère' (the lights), as opposed to the tank units which were referred to as 'la lourde' (the heavies, with a certain amount of friendly rivalry). An AML commander was thus known as a 'chef de voiture' or car commander instead of tank

commander. Because of the very lightness of these CLB regiments, they could be flown to any point within the range of the French Armée de l'Air's transport aircraft in relays. As a result by the early 1970s these regiments were capable of being sent to intervene in a number of trouble spots in France's former African colonies and their personnel rapidly became among the army's most experienced troops.

Generally the CLB regiments were organised in three (and later four) escadrons, or squadrons. Each escadron was made up of a command platoon with a single AML 60 and support vehicles, three armoured car platoons, a 'commando' platoon equivalent roughly to the assault troop found in British armoured car regiments made up of portée infantry in 4 x 4 trucks and a support platoon including a light recovery section and supply vehicles. Each armoured car platoon included three AML H60s (including an AML H60-12), two AML H90s and four Hotchkiss Jeeps. These were crewed by a total of one officer, five NCOs and twenty-one other ranks.

CLB regiments were not the only units in the French Army equipped with AMLs. The army's relatively small number of professional regiments, normally selected when overseas intervention was required, included elements trained to employ the AML due to its ease of deployment. These included the Régiment d'Infanterie-Chars de Marine (RICM), which received its first AMLs in 1963 at Vannes, the

LEFT The battalion commander of the 5ème Régiment de Chasseurs leads the 1965 Bastille Day Parade at Périgueux in the Dordogne in an AML 60-7 but with no mortar in the turret. This vehicle is typical of the first batch of AMLs. During the sixties, the 5ème Régiment de Chasseurs was equipped with a mix of AMLs and Ferrets (Mk 1 and Mk 2). The full replacement of the Ferret did not happen until the beginning of the 1970s within the French Army.

1er Régiment de Hussards Parachutistes (1er RHP) based at Tarbes and the 1er Régiment Étranger de Cavalerie (1er REC) when in garrison at Orange. These units did not always share the regimental structure employed by the DOT regiments on French soil.

On many occasions between 1970 and 1990 small French units were sent to Equatorial Africa and Lebanon in fulfilment of defence agreements, on UN mandates or at the request of local governments faced with insurrection. The French Army organised a number of units of professional soldiers in order to permit their use outside NATO commitments with minimal complications. These units, which included elements of several armoured units, formed the Force d'Action Rapide. In the Arme Blindée Cavalerie these units included the RICM, 1er Régiment de Hussards Parachutistes (RHP) and 1er Régiment Étranger de Cavalerie, which participated in the intervention in Chad and later in Lebanon.

The speedy and aggressive response of AML detachments often spelled the difference between success and disaster in military operations in Africa. On 3 February 1976 in Djibouti a military bus charged with picking up the children of French military personnel from school was hijacked by four terrorists in the Ambouli area. It was driven towards the Loyada border crossing on the Somali frontier, 18km away. Some accounts describe six terrorists and state that the men were Somalis

with the political aim of incorporating Djibouti into Somalia. Some 33 hostages were taken, including 31 elementary school-aged children. The French military forces in the area were alerted immediately. The bus broke down mere

BELOW Named after some long forgotten battle from the French war in Indochina, 'DINH KHE' is manned by troops of the Régiment d'Infanterie-Chars de Marine (RICM). During the time of National Service, conscripts were not obliged to serve outside Metropolitan France or NATO countries. Accordingly, there were several regiments comprised solely of professional soldiers such as RICM and of course the Foreign Legion for deployment overseas. These units formed the basis of French Intervention Forces that were invariably committed to areas of crisis across Africa with the essential requirement that they be air transportable at short notice.

ABOVE The French Army has supported numerous United Nations peace-keeping operations such as UNIFIL – the United Nations Interim Force In Lebanon. On 2 May 1978, PLO fighters attacked the French base near Tyre and ambushed a convoy of UN soldiers close by. Here, an RICM AML 60-12 of 1er Escadron de Combat returns fire against the PLO. During the firefight, two French soldiers including one 'Marsouin' were killed and several wounded, including the overall French commander, Col Jean Germain Salvan. Note that this AML is equipped with infrared driving headlights beside the un-ditching channels.

metres away from the border crossing in French-held territory. The 2nd Company of the 2ème Régiment Étranger de Parachutistes and the 13ème Demi-Brigade de Légion Étrangère's Escadron de Reconnaissance in AMLs deployed instantly to seize the roadways adjacent to the Loyada border post to stop the terrorists escaping with the hostages into Somalia.

On the opposite side of the border, Somali troops took up armed positions while night fell. The AMLs were employed to stand off and to restrict any support from Somalia. The following day a team of elite snipers from the Gendarmerie Nationale's GIGN anti-terror unit took up positions with Legion snipers overlooking the bus. In the night the terrorists had been reinforced from the Somali side of the border and their intentions were unknown. One child hostage was abducted into Somalia, although liberated some time later. The French reinforced their own with a Gendarmerie Mobile squadron. General Brasart, the commander of the Territoire Francais des Afars et des Issas took over direction of the situation on 4 February. He determined that the bus would be taken by assault as soon as possible. The sniper teams opened fire on the terrorists at 15.45hrs while the AML squadron prepared to open fire on any Somali transgression of the frontier. Their mission was to protect the hostage rescue from any Somali incursion.

As soon as the légionnaires began their assault on the bus, the Somali regulars opened fire on the French. The AML squadron

neutralised each Somali position in turn, covering the 2ème Compagnie's rescue, which was successfully concluded within 20 minutes. At 16.05hrs the action was finished. Five hostages including the bus driver and assistant had been wounded during the rescue. Tragically a little girl was killed by one of the terrorists during the rescue, and another child died several days later in Paris after being airlifted out. Seven terrorists were killed in the incident, and Lt Doucet of the 2ème Compagnie, 2ème REP was wounded during the gun battle. Losses among the Somali regulars across the border were never confirmed, but it is certain that they would have intervened in the rescue had the reconnaissance squadron's AMLs not been available to dissuade them.

In 1975, the French units serving in Chad were repatriated at the request of President Malloum. The Forces Armées Tchadiennes were rapidly faced by a Lybian-funded insurrection that gained control in large areas of northern Chad. Bardai and Zouar fell to the rebels in 1977, and Faya fell in early 1978. The Chadian government appealed to France to intervene. The speed with which the French dispatched forces to intervene in Chad was remarkable. One unit that saw much action in Chad in 1978 was the Regiment d'Infanterie-Chars de la Marine (RICM), another was the 1er Régiment de Hussards Parachutistes. Finally two heavy armoured regiments, the 4ème Régiment de Dragons and the 501ème Régiment de Chars de Combat, each maintained professional squadrons which could be deployed in AMLs (and on at least one occasion with AMX 30Bs) to Africa.

The first of the 2ème Escadron, RICM's AML platoons, was flown into the chaos in Chad around 24 hours after the request was made and were sent into action immediately, followed by a platoon from the 1er REC from Orange which landed in Transalls at Moussono a few hours later. One of these units had been alerted mere hours before take-off, a commendable level of readiness in any army. By 19 April, the rest of the two squadrons were in Chad, fighting rebel forces around the town of Salal. An RICM crewman recalled:

'We advanced into Salal as part of a group of 8 AMLs. About 2km from the objective we encountered the enemy in company strength;

RIGHT The RICM is the most highly decorated unit in the French Army and is manned solely by professional soldiers so is a vital component of French Intervention Forces, particularly in Africa. Founded in August 1914 at the outbreak of the First World War, it is heir to the Régiment d'Infanterie Coloniale du Maroc with which it shares the initials RICM. It thus continues the proud tradition of French colonial troops that were known derisively as 'Marsouins' or 'Porpoises' by the rest of the French Army, but to the regiment it became a badge of honour. This is reflected in the outline of a porpoise at the end of the vehicle names inscribed on the turret sides above the regimental insignia on the hull sides.

about 150 well-armed and determined rebels holding positions in twos and threes behind the sand dunes. Our first shots hit their ammunition lorry. We split up, the two 1er REC cars attacked Fort Salal while our six attacked the rebel infantry. Our squadron commander's AML ditched in soft ground and was literally swarmed by rebels, who pried open the hatches and managed to shoot the driver and gunner. The rest of the AMLs shot the insurgents off the

BELOW An ostrich ambles past a line of AMLs from the RICM near N'Djamena, capital city of Chad, in 1983 during Operation 'Manta'. This operation involved around 3,500 French military personnel including fighter and ground-attack aircraft as well as helicopter gunships with troops flown in from France and the Central African Republic. At the time it was the most significant deployment of the French Army since the Algerian conflict. Operation 'Manta' was undertaken to counter the invasion of Chad by 11,000 troops of Colonel Qaddafi's Libyan Army. The conflict ended with a Franco-Libyan accord that left Qaddafi's troops occupying a significant amount of territory in northern Chad.

'At the beginning of 1986 I deployed with my platoon from the 1er Escadron, 4ème Régiment de Dragons (RD) to the Central African Republic. Mine was a specialised detachment, for the 4e RD included a squadron of professional soldiers, one of only two such squadrons in two regiments in the cavalry (and both were normally equipped with AMX 30 series MBTs). Ours was a conscript army in those days, and in the 1e Escadron 4ème RD we were unique in that we were qualified to crew the army's newest tank, the AMX 30 B2, as well as the Panhard AML. To keep our training

BELOW The AML 60-7 of Lt Thomas Seignon as commander of the AML peloton of 1er Escadron, 4ème Régiment de Dragons, at the unit's base near Bangui, capital of the Central African Republic, in the spring of 1986. This vehicle is named 'BOUAR' and is a command vehicle, discernible by the twin radio antennae, there being no room inside an AML 90 for such a radio installation. Named after a market town in the Central African Republic, 'BOUAR' is painted in white letters on a black solid background with the company crest above on the turret sides. A regimental crest sticker is displayed on the left front part of the vehicle hull.

fresh we attached a platoon of AMLs to the 1er Escadron on a permanent basis, where they served alongside our 17 AMX 30 B2s. We could deploy at any given time to engage adversaries very different from the armoured forces of the Warsaw Pact, our anticipated enemy at the time. Alerted to the eventuality of leading my platoon of AMLs to the Central African Republic in September 1985, I spent the next months training the crews as best as could be managed in cold to freezing temperatures. When we arrived in Africa in temperatures of 35 degrees Celsius and in humidity approaching 90% we naturally had to adjust.

'After a short but vital acclimatisation period we set ourselves up in a small compound in the heart of the capital, Bangui. The platoon was made up of five AMLs – three AML 90s, an AML 60-12 for the platoon sergeant (which is the rough anglicisation for the French adjoint de peloton – the rank actually was a maréchal des logis in the cavalry) – and my own AML 60-7 command car. Four Jeeps and two supply lorries completed the effectives. My orders left me some considerable autonomy in selecting my range areas and training areas. I was able to quickly organise several platoon exercises within dozens of kilometres of the capital, and on one of these I led half my platoon – two AML 90s, my AML 60-7, two Jeeps and a lorry out on patrol 50km north of Bangui.

'We spent the morning in a coordinated series of movements with the Army Aviation's Gazelle flight, and without the constraints of highly populated European training areas, the helicopter pilots really showed off their low-level flying skills. One pilot repeatedly demonstrated that he could actually touch our wireless antennae with his landing skids. We spent the afternoon advancing towards our base in the capital, and I decided upon attempting a return to base via a secondary axis. A secondary axis in our military jargon meant in local terms a dirt track, in large part impassable to vehicles (as we found). The car commander leading the column soon found himself stopped in front of a village by an inhabitant who identified himself as the village head man. I drove up to the front of the column as I knew that in this part of Africa custom dictated that a chief would only speak to his opposite number.

'My linguistic capabilities in the local dialect being even more limited than the chief's in the language of Molière, it took quite some time to figure out a way to understand each other. He made me to understand that nearby there stood a lake of sorts, replete with crocodiles, which could only be discerned by their eyes protruding above the still surface. These crocodiles, I realised, were vicious creatures who had recently killed one of the village's children. The chief asked me to dispose of the crocodiles with my platoon's AML 90s. I had some difficulty explaining to him that France's mission in the area did not include culling wild animal populations. I had already been challenged in my ecological convictions a couple of days earlier when my smiling sergeant had triumphantly brought in a harvest of coconuts obtained by shooting up a coconut tree in stages of 9mm, 5.56mm FAMAS fire before chopping the whole tree down finally in a burst of 12.7mm from his AML 60-12.

'Back in 1986 we certainly did not take environmental issues as seriously as we might

RIGHT Regimental Crest of the 4ème Régiment de Dragons with the motto 'Je Boute Avant' or 'I Charge Forward', since in previous incarnations the crest incorporated a ferocious sanglier or wild boar.

today, but all the same I was unwilling to inflict any ecological disasters on any part of the local population (human or animal). I politely declined the chief's request that we massacre the crocodiles, which took some three hours. I led my column away to the primary axis, my topographical exercise in tatters … chastened in the knowledge that in Africa we were the ones wearing the watches, but the locals were the ones who had time – all the time they wanted.'

BELOW This rear view of 'BOUAR' shows the registration plate of Tricolor 234 0197 on the left and the standard NATO tactical sign of a rectangular white stencil with PB (Peloton Blindée) at top left and EFAO (Éléments Français d'Assistance Opérationnelle) at lower right. This is repeated on the front right wing as is the registration plate at the lower hull front.

BELOW Sporting the distinctive three colour camouflage scheme of green, brown and black adopted late in its career, the Panhard AML was withdrawn from frontline service with the French Army in 1991 but the Foreign Legion continued to use it for many more years in various parts of Africa. A total of 210 AML 90s and 425 AML 60s was procured by the French Army while the Gendarmerie bought 45 AML 90s and 70 AML 60s. In French service, the AML underwent few modifications or improvements beyond the adoption of the improved GIAT Industries APFSDS ammunition that necessitated a modified muzzle brake and recoil system. With a muzzle velocity of 1,050m/s, the APFSDS round can penetrate 50mm of conventional steel at 1,300m.

stricken vehicle with machine-gun fire, closing the distance and rescuing the captain who had been shot through the hand. The rebel attack was broken and the survivors were driven off.'

In another incident at Katafa, AMLs from the 2ème Escadron RICM patrolling the road from Abéché to Oum Hadger encountered 100 rebels, and in the ensuing firefight 16 rebels were killed and 3 rebels were captured. The 1er REC AML squadron relieved the 2ème Escadron RICM at Abéché and continued on internal security operations patrolling the area stretching from Ati, to N'Djamena and Mao. On 20 May 1978 the 1er REC's AML platoons drove insurgents out of Ati in conjunction with the RICM's AMLs and Chadian infantry. Through the remainder of 1978 and into 1979, the RICM and 1er REC's AML platoons operated in Chad in rotations of four to six months, with regular reliefs from professional cadres from the 4ème Régiment de Dragons and the 501ème RCC. The AML platoons served as intervention forces capable of moving quickly and striking decisively at rebel incursions.

On 19 May 1978 at Kolwezi, a battalion of 415 paratroopers from the 2ème Régiment Étranger de Parachutistes executed a combat drop into the town to rescue a large number of African and European hostages. As soon as they landed they realised that their enemy was well organised and ironically included a platoon of stolen Zairian AML 60s (manned by Katangan deserters from the Zairian Army). These same rebels had already crushed an attempt by the Zairian Army to land paratroopers the previous day and the AMLs were considered a serious threat. Legion paratroopers destroyed one of the AML 60s with LRAC rocket launcher fire within the first hours of landing as it led a determined Katangan counter-attack. A second

was destroyed that night during brutal fighting. The remainder of the 2e REP landed on 20 May at dawn, Belgian para-commandos reinforced the French bridgehead the following morning and the area was secured.

During its deployments in Africa the AML demonstrated its strategic mobility, simplicity and firepower on many occasions in Africa, where a number of units had detachments assigned in semi-permanence in the later years of the 20th century. The armoured platoon (including three AML H60s and two AML H90s) assigned to the Eléments Français d'Assistance Opérationnelle (EFAO) in the Central African Republic stationed in Bangui from 1979 to 1998 is a good example. Additionally, the AML was an important component of reserve territorial armoured units, made up of stored vehicles for the most part with a kernel of operational machines crewed by detachments from active CLB units. The AML was also a vital part of the internal security apparatus available to the French government, serving as partial equipment of the Groupement Blindé de Gendarmerie Mobile (GBGM) based at Satory until their replacement by the VBC 90 at the end of the 1980s.

The AML was withdrawn from French service in 1991, the last two regiments being so equipped were the 1er Régiment de Hussards Parachutistes and the 4ème Régiment de

ABOVE Operation 'Noroît' was launched in October 1990 to protect and evacuate French nationals from Rwanda following the outbreak of civil war between the Hutus and the Tutsis. The primary aim of the operation was to secure the airport at the capital Kigali to allow the evacuation of vulnerable civilians. Armour support was provided by the AML armoured cars of the RICM (note the regimental insignia on the turret side) and they undertook two reconnaissance missions to Butare on 27 and 28 October and to Ruhengeri and Gisenyi on 30 and 31 October to clear road blocks hampering movement towards the capital. This weather-beaten AML 90 takes part in the evacuation of Ruhengeri in January 1991 when 300 people, including 185 French, were escorted to Kigali following an attack by Tutsi fighters of the Rwanda Patriotic Front.

Chasseurs; elsewhere they were replaced by the ERC 90 and AMX 10 RC in the regiments that survived the army reorganisations of 1977, 1984 and following the end of the Cold War. Today only the 4ème RCh, 1er RHP, 1er REC and the RICM are still in the French Army's order of battle. The AML 60 and AML 90 gave sterling service and were great favourites with their French crews. All this in spite of its thin armour, its mediocre performance in nocturnal combat and its all-road rather than all-terrain performance.

The modern French Army from Napoleon onwards has always been innovative, especially with the Arme Blanche. Mobility, protection and firepower have been stressed causing light, reconnaissance and striking cavalry in the shape of chasseurs, lancers and hussars to be

LEFT The AML continued in service with the French Army until 2012. The very last ones were painted in an experimental urban camouflage scheme to act as OPFOR (or Opposition Forces) at the Urban Area Training Centre (CENZUB) located in Sissonne in eastern France.

developed as well as heavier shock troops – cuirassier and dragoons.

Their evolution is clear: from nimble, mounted troopers as comfortable on foot with a carbine as they were in the saddle with a sabre, came the French tradition of light armoured vehicles. Carefully trained, enterprising and determined crews who understood the agility of a wheeled, armoured vehicle combined with remarkably heavy firepower was the result. While Ney, Marmont and May would not have recognised the Panhard Automitrailleuse Légère, they would immediately have understood its genesis and purpose.

The units shown in the panel (left) were equipped with the AML series in the French Army during 1982.

French Army units equipped with the AML series, 1982

- 4ème Régiment de Hussards based at Laon – 8ème Division d'Infanterie at Amiens.
- 4ème Régiment de Chasseurs based at La Valbonne – 27ème Division d'Infanterie Alpine at Grenoble.
- 5ème Régiment de Chasseurs based at Périgueux – 15ème Division d'Infanterie at Limoges.
- 7ème Régiment de Chasseurs based at Arras – 12ème Division d'Infanterie at Rouen.
- 1er Régiment Etranger de Cavalerie based at Orange – 14ème Division d'Infanterie at Lyon.
- 1er Régiment de Hussards Parachutistes based at Tarbes – 11ème Division Parachutistes at Toulouse.
- Régiment d'Infanterie-Chars de Marine based at Vannes – 9ème Division d'Infanterie de la Marine at Nantes.
- Groupement Blindé de Gendarmerie Mobile based at Satory.

French Army reserve units equipped with the AML, 1982

- 9ème Régiment de Chasseur – reserve cadre from 5ème RCh.
- 13ème Régiment de Chasseurs – reserve, cadre from 4ème RCh.
- 3ème Régiment de Chasseurs – mixed EBR and AML training unit supporting the EAABC at Saumur, based at Fontevraud.
- 6ème Régiment de Chasseurs – reserve regiment with pre-positioned equipment at the Chartres CM 101 mobilisation centre.
- 12ème Régiment de Dragons – reserve regiment with pre-positioned equipment at the Pannes CM 108 mobilisation centre.
- 29ème Régiment de Dragons – reserve regiment with pre-positioned equipment at the Provins CM 29 mobilisation centre.

AML production

The development and procurement of the Automitrailleuse Légère was sponsored by the French Ministry of Defence, Délégation Générale pour l'Armement and Direction des Armements Terrestres through the Direction Centrale du Matériel de l'Armée de Terre and the French Army. The main manufacturer was the Sociéte de Constructions Mécaniques Panhard et Levassor of the Avenue d'Ivry, Paris, with major subcontractors including

OPPOSITE Panhard's successor to the AML 90 was the ERC 90 or Engin á Roues, Canon Sagaie (the French word for 'assegai', an African stabbing spear). The French armed forces procured 190 ERC 90 Sagaie from 1984 and it became the standard AFV of the French Rapid Deployment Force. This Sagaie served with Peloton Rimbert of 1er Régiment Étrangere Cavalerie. Note the French and Foreign Legion pennants flying at the radio antennae, during Operation 'Manta' in Mali in 1983.

ABOVE Although three times heavier than the AML 90, the ERC 90 Sagaie is air-transportable in a C-160 Transall or C-130 Hercules as shown here with 'CASTIGLIONE' reversing into a Transall, although only one vehicle can be carried at a time. The Sagaie commemorates the victory of the French Army of Italy under General Napoleon Bonaparte over Hapsburg Austria in 1796.

RIGHT Against a background of M3 VTTs, the turret of an AML 60-12 is lowered into the hull during the final stages of assembly.

RIGHT AND FAR RIGHT The manufacture of the AML series was initially undertaken at Panhard's traditional automobile factory at 18 Avenue de la Porte d'Ivry in the XIII district of Paris, with a production line of AML 60s (right) and spray painting (far right).

LEFT A line of 90mm F1 turrets at CNMP (Compagnie Normande de Mécanique de Précision) Berthiez facility in Le Havre. AHE (Ateliers du Havre) ceased its production activities in 1963 when it was taken over by SNECMA (Société Nationale d'Etudes et de Construction de Moteurs d'Aviation) up to 1966 and thereafter by CNMP-Berthiez.

Hispano Suiza, Peugeot, Societe d'Applications des Machines Motrices and Thomson-DASA Armements – Thomson-Brandt. As of 1 January 1997, a total of 6,237 Automitrailleuse Légère and Eland vehicles had been manufactured together with a further 1,180 M3 VTT APCs. In 1997, the Automitrailleuse Légère 90 vehicle had a unit price of $373,700. This price could vary significantly depending on the weapon systems or other options selected by the customer. The Eland was built under licence by Sandock Austral of Benoni, near Johannesburg, in the Republic of South Africa and subsequently by Reumech OMC, formerly Reumech Sandock Limited.

BELOW New Eland armoured cars are put through their paces on the Sandock Austral test track at Boksburg near Johannesburg.

Chapter Three

Anatomy of the AML and Eland

Rea Cullivan

Like all the best armoured fighting vehicle designs, the Panhard AML combined the virtues of simplicity and versatility that universally won the affection and esteem of their crews. As a leading specialist in the Panhard AML and Eland armoured cars, Rea Cullivan compiled this chapter and relates the technical aspects and foibles of this quintessentially French design.

OPPOSITE Most of the elements of a reconnaissance platoon prepare to move out on patrol with the AML 60-7 at left, the AML 90 at right and the Hotchkiss M201 and Renault Camion at the rear.

ABOVE The first batch of production AML 60s awaits delivery to the French Army in 1961 with the first unit to receive them in Metropolitan France being the 2ème Hussards. Other AMLs were immediately dispatched to Algeria in December but arrived too late to have any impact on the conflict that ended in March 1962. These vehicles have the early pattern tyres, single spotlight on the turret and lack un-ditching channels.

BELOW To enhance its tactical mobility, the basic models of the AML series can be fitted with floatation equipment to allow them to negotiate rivers and waterways with the minimum of preparation (the vehicle below is an AML HS-30). One of the design criteria for the original AML was that the vehicle was to be amphibious but this requirement compromised the basic design to an unacceptable degree.

AML technical description

In 1959, Panhard presented its first prototype of the Automitrailleuse Légère armoured car in response to French Army needs. The original order for 2,000 vehicles was pre-empted by the French decision to fabricate and deploy an embryonic nuclear force structure under President de Gaulle. This action reduced the French order to 600 units, as funding for almost all conventional programmes was reduced drastically by the priorities given to French nuclear forces or Force de Frappe. Panhard started a strong foreign sales effort that resulted in the AML family of vehicles becoming the worldwide market leader in armoured cars.

In terms of strategic mobility the AML represented a major watershed in French armoured vehicle development, owing to its combination of lightweight and high speed. It could attain speeds of up to 90kmh on tar or packed gravel. The vehicle also had an exceptional road range of 600km. Its fuel tank had a capacity of 156 litres (34.3 Imperial gallons) and fuel consumption hovered around a modest 25 litres/100km. It could negotiate obstacles up to 0.3m in height, climb 60% gradients and 30% side slopes, and ford streams to a depth of 1.1m without special preparation. Permanent four-wheel drive and an independent suspension allowed for optimal cross-country performance. An AML could also clear a trench up to 3.1m in width with the use of sand channels. Standard equipment included the sand channels, two turret-mounted searchlights, four run-flat tyres with nitrogen inner tubes plus one spare, a complete set of tools, and a full range of day vision equipment. The electrical system was a 24-volt system employing two 12-volt batteries in series, which were situated behind the driver in the centre of the hull just forward of the turret.

The AML continued in production with few modifications until the late 1980s, at which time its range of optional equipment had come to include infrared and image intensification vision devices, updated fire control system, air conditioning, an amphibious kit, and an NBC ventilation system which safeguarded the crew from the effects of nuclear fallout as well as biological or chemical weapons. During an era when many of these features were becoming standard on armoured fighting vehicles, the relative austerity of the AML was often commented on. However, it was Panhard's policy to let its customers specify the exact degree of equipment to be fitted, according to their particular needs and budget. Indeed, at one time no two shipments of AMLs delivered to foreign export clients were ever exactly the same. It was this versatility which allowed the AML's basic concept to be further refined into innumerable variants, as well as the related Eland derivative.

It remains unclear how many AMLs were produced, although the number is believed to be upwards of 4,000. In June 1994, Panhard stated that it had manufactured 6,025 AMLs and M3 VTTs.

AML hull and turret

A squat, compact, armoured vehicle, the AML possesses a sharply angled hull that slopes downwards towards the front and less prominently at the rear. In terms of layout the hull resembles an elongated octagon tapering to a small nose plate at the front. The sloped front of the hull is almost contiguous with the base of the turret ring and avoids the vulnerabilities of an exposed horizontal roof line or shot traps.

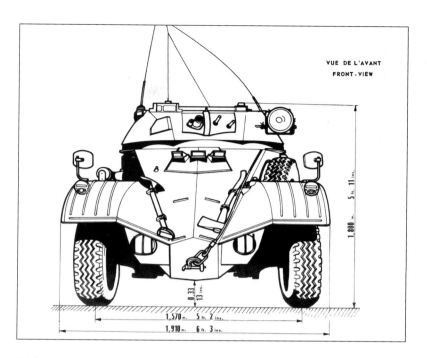

ABOVE The front hull configuration of the AML 60-7.

BELOW AML Type 245 loading plan.

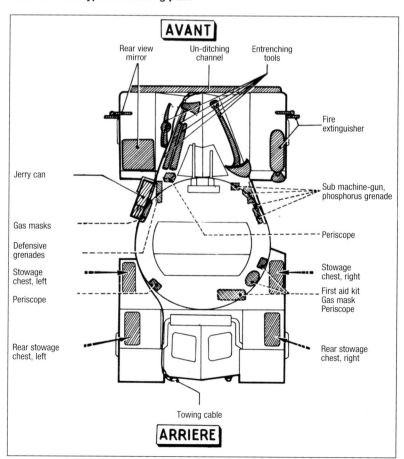

to each rear wheel. Sand or un-ditching channels are stowed across the lower hull front and the headlamps are located on each side of the towing shackle, beneath the channels. The engine bay is completely enclosed in the hull rear, with air intake and exhaust openings. It is insulated from the crew compartment by a removable bulkhead and accessed through two hinged panels in the rear hull.

A stripped AML hull bereft of any turret or equipment weighs about 3,620kg (3.6 tonnes). It is 3.6m in length, 1.7m in width, and just 1m in height. The hull is fabricated from thirteen pieces of welded homogenous plate steel varying in thickness from 8mm to 12mm with the exception of the glacis plate, which is up to 30mm thick in the last production models. This provides the crew with modest protection from grenades, shell fragments, and small-arms fire up to 7.62mm ball at any angle and 7.62mm armour-piercing ammunition at most angles. AML hulls have the maximum thickness of the armour plate on the glacis and nose, with reduced protection on the rear surfaces of the hull and the hull floor, as is conventional

ABOVE The rear compartment of the AML with the Panhard 4HD 90hp air-cooled petrol engine.

There is a large inverted 'V' glacis plate at the front of the hull in which the driver's hatch opening is located. The AML may be readily identified by its sizeable semicircular wheel arches and the external stowage bins adjacent

RIGHT Each door has stowage for a fire extinguisher, first-aid kit and the crew's personal weapons of a MAT-49 sub-machine-gun.

FAR RIGHT Each side door is configured to allow the crew to use it as a shield against enemy fire while disembarking. The left-hand door opens forwards to provide cover from the front while the other opens rearwards to give cover from behind, giving the crew the choice of escape depending on where enemy fire is coming from.

in any AFV design. As a countermeasure against land mines, the hull floor consists of two plates welded together to form a shallow, flat vee shape to deflect blasts away from the crew. This proved more than adequate with regards to the anti-personnel mines and small, rudimentary explosive devices that were a common fixture of the insurgents the French Army encountered in Algeria and Indochina. It was considerably less effective against the proliferation of cheap anti-tank mines that began appearing in the hands of insurgent armies during the late 1960s, however.

There is an entry door on each side of the hull, the left one normally being reserved for emergency purposes only. A spare tyre is mounted on the exterior of the left door as standard, although this location has been used to stow a host of other items as well, including spare fuel or water cans, or a fire extinguisher. Above both doors, the hull widens into a circular flange to accommodate the turret. While this feature allows for wider turrets to be bolted on to the somewhat narrow hull, it also restricts the size of the turret basket.

The driver is seated in a central position at the front of the hull in a very restricted space and observes the environment through a single hatch cover located in the glacis plate, or through three integral periscopes when in

ABOVE Driver's compartment of AML 60.

BELOW Driver's panel.

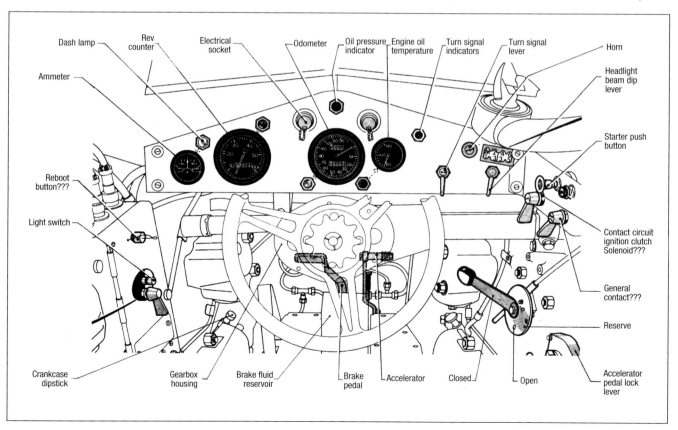

Dash lamp — Rev counter — Electrical socket — Odometer — Oil pressure indicator — Engine oil temperature — Turn signal indicators — Turn signal lever — Horn

Ammeter — Headlight beam dip lever

Reboot button??? — Starter push button

Light switch — Contact circuit ignition clutch Solenoid???

General contact???

Reserve

Crankcase dipstick — Gearbox housing — Brake fluid reservoir — Brake pedal — Accelerator — Closed — Open — Accelerator pedal lock lever

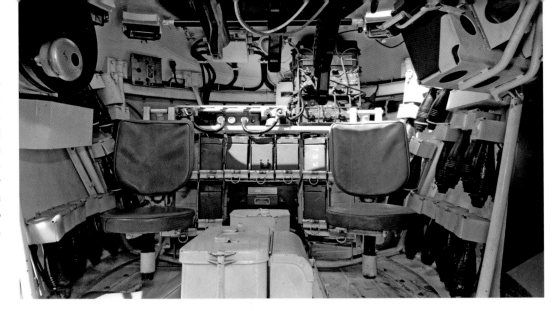

RIGHT Turret interior of an AML 60-7 looking rearwards, with 60mm mortar bombs stowed around the hull sides and boxes of machine-gun ammunition below the turret ring, with the wireless set at top right.

RIGHT AND BELOW The interior of the AML turret is cramped by any standards with the machine-guns intruding significantly inside. The commander has several duties to perform, mostly simultaneously, including observation outside the vehicle; monitoring the radio net; directing the gunner with range and target information; passing the 60mm mortar bombs to the gunner and serving the twin machine-guns, as well as constantly guiding the driver.

RIGHT AML turret mounting the latter Brandt 60mm Long Range Gun-Mortar.

CENTRE Configuration of AML 60-7 turret with twin 7.5mm co-axial machine-guns.

combat. The centre periscope piece can be replaced as required by an infrared or night vision periscope to facilitate night driving.

Immediately to the driver's rear is the turret, which seats the vehicle commander on the left and the gunner to the right. The commander conducts surveillance, acquires targets, makes the necessary ranging and ordnance calculations, and directs the gunner accordingly. He is also responsible for loading the main armament, and the radio and telecom system. The gunner is seated on the right side of the turret and operates the main and co-axial armament, as well as the roof-mounted searchlight. When the commander specifies a target, the gunner manually traverses and elevates the main armament by hand wheels. The commander and gunner are each provided with single-piece hatch covers opening to the front or rear. They may open the hatches and elevate their seats for increased situational awareness when not otherwise engaged. During combat, each may continue to observe the terrain from the protection of the turret through four removable L794B periscopes in front of their respective hatches. There are minor variations in the number of periscopes installed, depending on the turret model. Like the hull, the turret is of all-welded construction, and varies in thickness from 7mm at the rear to 14mm of steel at the turret front. Some turrets may incorporate heavier armour plate with a maximum thickness of up to 20mm. There are two electrically operated smoke dischargers on each side of the turret.

Two turrets were initially supplied with the AML, one mounting a combination of a 60mm mortar and twin 7.5mm machine-guns, and the other a 90mm gun and a single 7.5mm machine-gun. Both were manufactured by the CNMP-Berthiez Corporation and were classified as the HE 60-7 and H90 turrets, respectively. Due to the limited space in the AML's hull, all ammunition had to be carried in the turret.

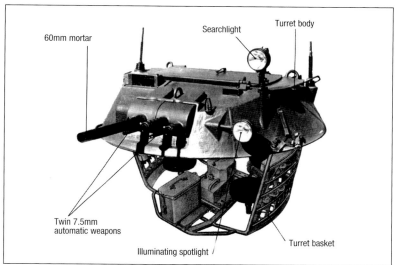

BELOW Configuration of AML 60-12 turret with co-axial 12.7mm heavy machine-gun.

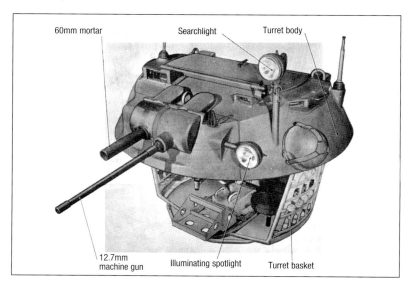

59

ANATOMY OF THE AML AND ELAND

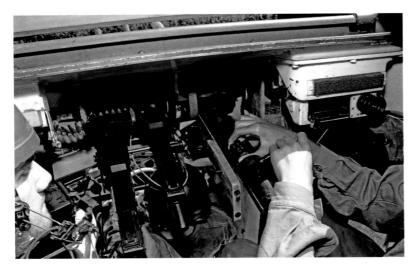

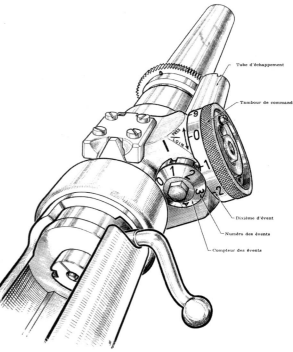

The breech-loading Brandt Modèle CM60A1 was the original weapon fitted to the AML 60. It has a range of 300m in the direct firing mode and 3,000m for indirect fire. In action its most important role was to produce smoke, either as a screen or to mark targets and to provide illumination at night.

The HE 60-7 turret appeared in 1959 and carries a 60mm Hotchkiss-Brandt CM60A1/ Model HB 60 mortar on the right and twin co-axial M1952 (AA Mle 52) machine guns on the left. It weighs 1,180kg. The gunner has a combined M112/3 monocular telescope and binocular periscope with a magnification of x 5. Elevation aiming control is linked to the mortar but manual scanning is also possible.

Access to the 44 stowed mortar bombs was efficient with the rounds mostly being stored in the turret basket floor (turntable). There are 15 ready 60mm high-explosive projectiles stowed in a bin on a rack towards the front of the turntable, with another 23 stowed vertically in holders around the turntable. There are also two separate bins on either side of the crew's wireless radio set for specialised ammunition such as illuminating

and smoke projectiles. Each of these bins holds an additional three rounds. Machine gun ammunition is stowed in 16 boxes of 200 rounds each for a total of 3,200 7.5mm rounds. There are slight differences in the amount of ammunition carried, depending on the type of radio equipment fitted.

The CM60A1 possesses an opening breech locked by a falling block, much like direct fire artillery. It can be loaded either from the breech or muzzle and used in the direct role as needed. The mortar is mounted independently of the machine guns and is not an integral part of the turret, allowing it to be removed for servicing with relative ease. The co-axial machine guns have a maximum elevation of +50° and a depression of −15°, while the mortar has an elevation of +80° and a depression of −15°. In the direct fire role, the maximum range of

LEFT The Brandt 60mm Long Range Gun-Mortar has a range of 500m in the direct fire role and 5,000m for indirect fire. It is capable of high-angle fire for maximum effect in built-up areas and hilly terrain, making it especially suitable for irregular warfare. The AML 60 carries 31 to 50 60mm bombs depending on the wireless configuration and turret layout.

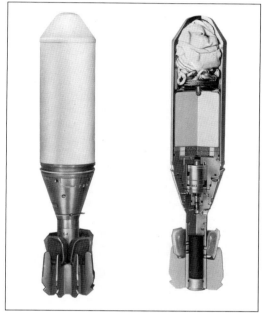

FAR LEFT Hotchkiss-Brandt 60mm bomb Mk 61 HE.

LEFT Hotchkiss-Brandt 60mm illuminating bomb Mk 63.

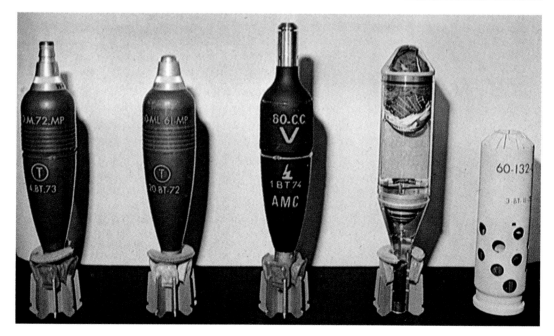

LEFT The types of enhanced rounds include high explosive (Mk 35-47 and Mk 72), Mk 63 illuminating, hollow charge anti-tank (OCCHB for Obus Charge Creuse Hotchkiss-Brandt), smoke and canister rounds. The weapon can be provided with either electrical or mechanical firing mechanisms.

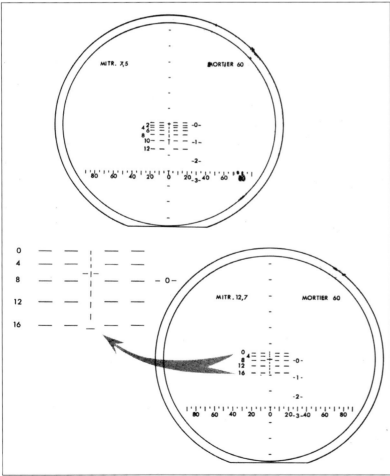

ABOVE The main supplementary weapon of the AML series was the Arme Automatique Transformable Modele 1952 or AA-52. Produced by the state concern Manufacture d'armes de Saint-Étienne, the machine-gun was used by both the infantry and the Arme Blindé Cavalerie, acquiring the nickname of La Nana – the Spanish for maid. Chambered for the 7.5mm x 54mm French cartridge, the AA-52 was designed following experiences in the French Indochina War where the armed forces used a multiplicity of weapons of different calibres causing severe logistical problems. The AA-52 continued in service into the 21st century although by then it had been re-chambered to take the standard NATO 7.62m x 51mm round whereupon it was designated NF-1. Early vehicle-mounted versions did not have the perforated cooling jacket as shown here on 'LINX'.

LEFT Periscope graticule for H60-7 (top) and H60-12 (bottom).

the CM60A1 is about 300m. This may be increased to up to 1,700m in the indirect fire role. AMLs carrying the HE 60-7 turret received the manufacturing code AML-245B but were known more commonly by their general service designation, AML-60.

Plans for the H90 turret were drawn up as early as 1959, although the first did not appear until 1960. It carries a 90mm DEFA D921/CN90F1 low-recoil gun on the right and a co-axial M1952 (AAT Mle 52) machine-gun on the left. The co-axial armament mounted parallel with the main gun helped establish range ballistically and aided in target correction when the low-velocity 90mm shells were being fired. The complete turret weighs 1,850kg. The gunner has a type M262 or M37 monocular telescopic sight with a fixed graticule and a magnification of x6. The gunner's eyepiece follows the gun in elevation or depression via a linkage mechanism. Both sights are adequate for locating and identifying targets at all ranges when daytime visibility permits. There is an optical ring sight that can be used by the gunner if his telescopic sight had been damaged. A modified M262 infrared sight and a PH-2-A infrared searchlight may be fitted retrospectively to all H90 turrets, enabling targets to be engaged at night as well.

THIS PAGE A sequence of photographs showing the replenishment of an AML 90 with 90mm ammunition.

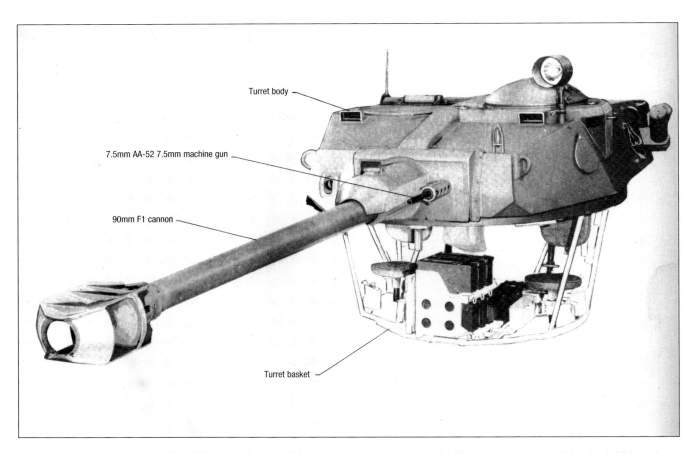

Turret body

7.5mm AA-52 7.5mm machine gun

90mm F1 cannon

Turret basket

ABOVE **Layout of H90 F1 turret.**

The H90 turret has sufficient stowage space to accommodate 30 main gun rounds. There are 10 90mm shells stowed vertically behind the gunner and another 10 behind the vehicle commander. Another 10 are stowed horizontally in double racks at the rear of the turret. Four types of 90mm ammunition could be carried: High Explosive (HE), High Explosive Anti-Tank (HEAT), smoke and canister. The HEAT round is especially light at only 7kg, making it easier to handle and load into the breech. An APFSDS round was also made available in the 1980s, although to fire this ammunition the gun had to be modified with a different recoil system and larger muzzle brake. Machine-gun ammunition is stowed in 10 boxes of 200 rounds each for a total of 2,000 7.5mm rounds.

The D921 gun recoils approximately 58cm during firing and is returned to its normal position by a hydro-pneumatic recuperator. It is fitted with a vertical sliding breech block which opens automatically upon gun runout and ejects the spent shell casing. The main gun is not stabilised in either azimuth or elevation. It has a maximum elevation of +15° and a depression of −8°. Effective range is 1,500m to 2,000m when firing HE and HEAT ammunition respectively. AMLs carrying the H90 turret received the manufacturing code AML-245C but were known more commonly by their general service designation, AML 90. The H90 turret was superseded in production by a heavily upgraded model known as the D-90 Lynx turret in 1978. AML 90s produced with this turret received the general service designation AML 90 Lynx.

AML engine and chassis

When the first AMLs rolled off the assembly line in 1960, they were powered by a 1.99-litre (1,997cc) Panhard Model 4HD air-cooled 4-cylinder petrol engine. This was a spark-ignition type modified from one developed for Panhard's successful range of 2-cylinder passenger cars. As was the case of the Panhard EBR heavy armoured car, a flat engine was favoured due to the restrictions imposed by the vehicle's compact hull and the need to conserve space within the limited dimensions of the rear engine compartment. The 4HD had

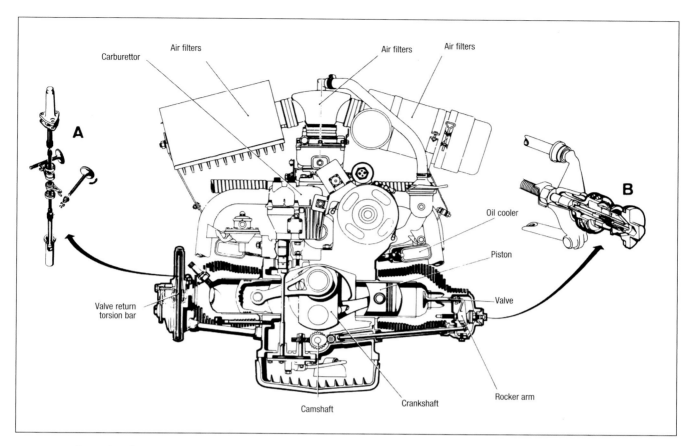

Air filters

Carburettor

Air filters

Air filters

A

B

Oil cooler

Piston

Valve

Rocker arm

Valve return
torsion bar

Camshaft

Crankshaft

a compression ratio of 7:1. It was capable of providing solid operational service for about 26,000km before major overhaul.

A pre-existing engine type had been selected as the basis for the 4HD because it was cheap and readily available when Panhard began work on the AML, reducing development and manufacturing costs. Development of a new engine between 1956 and 1959 would have left precious little time for the necessary test bed trials before it was installed in prototype vehicles. The 4HD's civilian industry counterpart was known as the X4, but it did not prove successful and was cancelled not long after Panhard's merger with Citroën later in the 1960s.

While the 4HD was more than adequate for its era, Panhard's export clients later called for more power, prompting the company to turn to a more efficient liquid-cooled Peugeot XD 3T diesel engine and make this optional beginning in 1980, after first redesigning the AML's rear hull and rear suspension in order to accommodate it. Power was increased by nearly 15% over the superseded 1.99-litre petrol engine and torque was up by 50%. Like the 4HD, the XD 3T was

developed with the civilian industry in mind and used a wide range of commercially available, off the shelf components to simplify maintenance. Some ten years later this same engine would appear in Panhard's VBL range of light scout cars. The XD 3T was also offered as part of a retrofit package for older production AMLs beginning in 1990, but surprisingly few countries took Panhard up on the offer, probably because it necessitated such an extensive and potentially costly rebuild of the rear hull.

The 4HD displaces 122cu in and is rated at 67kW (90hp) at 4,700rpm. It possesses a power-to-weight ratio of 12kW/tonne. The Panhard engine performed at its best in relatively dry, dust-free climates. It received some bad publicity in the 1970s, particularly when a number supplied to the Portuguese Army in Angola gave trouble in service. This appeared to be the result of excessively dusty operating conditions, which overwhelmed the inadequate air intakes and caused premature engine failure. The problem was rectified by the installation of modified custom-made air intakes, and the engines gave little difficulty thereafter.

ABOVE 1.99-litre (1,997cc) Panhard Model 4HD air-cooled flat 4-cylinder petrol engine. This sectional drawing shows details of the valve return on the left (A) and the hydraulic play adjustment on the right (B).

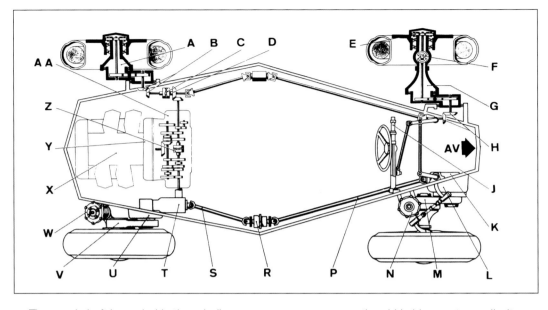

The crankshaft is carried in three ball bearings to reduce motor friction. A large cast aluminum fan is situated at the rear of the crankshaft to draw air over the engine cylinders before expelling it outside. Drive is transmitted from the engine to the gearbox by a centrifugal clutch with automatic control by electromagnet. This novel electric clutch eliminates the need for a clutch pedal, and is automatically disengaged when the driver of the vehicle grips the knob of the gearshift lever, which is located behind the driving position in the hull floor. The gearbox assembly is situated behind the clutch and has one reverse and six forward gears. It actually consists of two separate gearboxes, one for high and the other for low gear. The AML's low-range gearbox was designed for off-road use and has two low gears, a reverse gear and a top gear, while the high-range box is intended for road travel and has three low gears and one overdrive. When the low-range box is engaged, the high-range box remains in lowest gear and occupies the four gears of the upper gear range: sixth, fifth, fourth and third respectively.

The H-drive system was popular among wheeled armoured vehicles in the post-war period because it conserved hull space and gave them lower profiles. It also found favour among vehicles designed for internal security operations, as the drive system enabled it to keep moving even if wheels were damaged or lost due to land mines. In this regard the AML was no exception. It utilised what

was a conventional H-drive system, albeit with a patented Panhard innovation of two differentials rather than one central differential. Drive is directed from the gearbox along the hull by two universally jointed shafts – one on each side of the hull – towards the front wheels and by pinions towards the rear wheels. Both shafts drive a second cam-type differential that helps regulate speed between the front and rear wheels and effectively prohibits one pair of wheels from exerting a speed considerably different from that of the other. For example, the differentials will prevent one wheel pair from spinning if they lose traction on loose sand or muddy terrain. All four wheels are forced to rotate at the same speed as the others through a system which functions, in effect, as a limited slip differential. The incorporation of two differentials mitigated one of the chief disadvantages associated with the H-drive system, namely the tendency towards transmission torque wind-up and tyre scrub on roads.

The AML bears some interesting similarities with its predecessor in French service, the venerable Ferret scout car, in its transmission of drive from the gearbox by shafts to bevel boxes at each corner of the hull, and from thence to epicyclic final drives in the wheel hubs. There were a number of detail differences, however. Unlike the Ferret, drive is conveyed from the bevel boxes through an additional train of gears housed within cast trailing arms, upon which the wheels are mounted. The trailing arms form an integral part of the vehicle's suspension system and house a total of three double helical gears that in turn locate the wheels. At this point drive reaches the epicyclic hub reduction gears in the case of the rear wheels or is transmitted through a constant velocity joint to the front wheels. Panhard's decision to convey drive through internal gears in the trailing arms was influenced by the desire to make the AML chassis and hull as compact as possible; this system permitted the non-steered rear wheels to be located much closer to the hull and reduced the number of constant velocity joints used in the Ferret to articulate drive.

The front and rear wheels are sprung by coil springs with hydraulic telescopic dampers of the monotube design, which act on the trailing arms. The telescopic dampers contain a volume of pressurised nitrogen gas behind a floating piston to accommodate the piston rod when it enters the cylinder; the floating piston also separates the nitrogen from the hydraulic fluid. Each of the four wheels is fitted with 33cm Bendix drum brakes. The AML lacks power-assisted steering or power brakes, and only the front wheels are steered, in this case by a traditional rack and pinion mechanism.

The four Michelin 11.00 x 16-XL radial-ply tyres used on the AML are fitted with puncture-proof inner tubes. At zero inflation these tyres may operate up to 100km while travelling at a speed not exceeding 30kmh and still provide satisfactory traction on adverse terrain. The inner tubes are Hutchinson cellular VP-PVs, which contain a honeycomb complex of cells permanently inflated with nitrogen gas for run-flat purposes. The tyres are inflated to 31 and 42psi at the front and rear, respectively, for road operation; however, they may be deflated to as low as 10 and 16psi for driving on sand.

Eland technical description

With the end of the Algerian conflict, Panhard turned its attention to export clients in the hopes this would help create the economy of scale needed to keep production of the AML viable once pre-existing orders for the

ABOVE A trio of AML 60s advances across the desert with each following in the tracks of the others to minimise the risk of mines. Every AML is equipped with an air compressor to vary the tyre pressure depending on the terrain to be negotiated, thus tyres are partially deflated in soft sand conditions and re-inflated to normal for road use.

BELOW Eland Mk 7 with roof-mounted MG4 7.62mm machine-gun in the nutra colour scheme typical of South African AFVs that blends so well with the countryside.

French Army had been fulfilled. The company had no intention of forfeiting its investment to a relatively short and uneconomical production run, and needed hard currency to balance the cost of new research and development programmes. Thus, while numerous AMLs were being readied for shipment to North Africa in July 1961, they were being inspected by senior representatives of the South African Defence Force (SADF), then on a fact-finding mission to evaluate armoured cars from different countries and select one to re-equip the army. Panhard not only offered to sell them the AML, but also transfer the necessary technology and expertise to South Africa, which could then undertake local production.

In late 1960, the South African government had declared its intention to reduce its dependence on foreign arms suppliers. South Africa's Minister of Defence, Jacobus Johannes Fouché, instigated an investigation into the technical aspects and financial implications of manufacturing an armoured fighting vehicle locally. While South Africa had no experience producing heavy armour such as tanks, it had designed and built light armoured cars and other supporting vehicles in the past. The country had a long-standing tradition in the evolution of armoured cars on the African continent, going back to the Marmon-Herrington series of Second World War fame. South Africa had produced over 5,000 armoured cars in six variants during that conflict, and many had continued to see action during the post-war era. Fouché was convinced that South Africa's industrial and engineering base was sufficiently capable of mass-producing armoured cars again. His proposal was to commence assembly of a foreign design, and then continue developing a progressively larger percentage of its associated parts locally until the goal of a completely indigenous vehicle had been reached.

The fact that the AML had been developed for the Algerian theatre placed it in high standing with the visiting South African delegation, many of whose members had studied the counter-insurgency tactics employed there by French forces. This detail, coupled with the intrinsic advantages of the AML design, placed it in position to win the order for the South African Army. By November 1961 a production and licensing contract had been negotiated with Panhard. This called for 100 completed AMLs and enough turrets, engines, special tooling and other bulk parts for the later assembly of another 800 by a local contractor. It also sanctioned the domestic production of the AML chassis and hull in South African facilities.

Due to international controversy over South Africa's domestic policies at the time, Panhard's cooperation with the South African government was something of an open secret. For example, it declined to help South Africa set up an AML production line, but discreetly subcontracted the work to an eminent West German defence contractor, Henschel. When the first AMLs were delivered to the South African Army, all references to the manufacturer and French terminology were omitted. In official correspondence the AML was strictly described as the 'Vehicle A' by the South African government; the AML 60s and AML 90s imported from France or assembled from French hulls were classified as the VA Mk 1/60 and VA Mk 1/90, respectively.

In 1962, an assembly plant was established by Austral Iron and Engineering Works near Boksburg to begin assembling AMLs provided in kit form by Panhard. To cut down on development costs, Austral grafted local components into the Panhard kits wherever possible and designed its own parts where it found the imported ones inappropriate. The first prototype of the new Austral AML appeared in early 1963 and proved sufficiently successful that pilot production examples began to come off the lines at the Boksburg plant that July.

First to arrive was the Vehicle A Mk 2, and it was hoped this would supersede the original French-built Mk 1s in South African service. The VA Mk 2 models were almost impossible to distinguish from their French-built cousins, save for the lack of Panhard badging. The Mk 2s also replaced the 7.5mm AA-52 co-axial machine guns with the South African Browning M1919A4 .30-calibre machine guns rechambered for 7.62mm NATO ammunition. In 1966 they were withdrawn from service due to unspecified teething issues, and received a modified steering system on the front wheels. Only about 56 of these pilot production Mk 2s were delivered between 1963 and 1966.

Eland Mark 7. *(Artwork by Pierre Lowe Victor)*

1 Muzzle brake
2 Fire extinguisher
3 Brake fluid reservoir
4 Driver's hatch and visors
5 90mm Denel GT-2 gun
6 90mm ammunition racks (29 rounds in total)
7 L1000 7.62mm co-axial machine-gun

8 Main armament recuperators and breech assembly
9 Vehicle spotlight
10 Gunner's periscope
11 Gunner's hatch
12 L4 commander's 7.62mm machine-gun
13 Radio receiver set
14 Communications wire reel
15 Turret stowage bin

16 Turret 90mm ammunition rack
17 81mm smoker dischargers
18 Commander's cupola and vision blocks
19 General Motors 2.5-litre water-cooled petrol engine
20 Engine air cleaners
21 Spring diaphragm mechanical clutch

22 Turret basket
23 142-litre fuel tank
24 Jerrycan stowage rack
25 Electrical distribution box
26 Split rim wheels with Dunlop 12 x 16 Trak Grip tyres
27 Un-ditching channels
28 Driver's instrument panel
29 Shock absorber housing
30 Headlight

ABOVE Cpl William Surmon of A Squadron 1 Light Horse Regiment mans the commander's machine gun during Exercise 'Excalibur II' at the Army Battle School in Lohatla. The dependable Browning M1919A4 was designated the L4 in South African service after being rechambered for 7.62mm calibre ammunition. *(William Surman)*

The Mk 2 models were succeeded in 1967 by Mk 3s, which remained externally similar but incorporated a few minor alterations, such as a cable on the fuel cap, new wheel hubs, additional radio mounts and new brakes of local origin. At this point, Austral could reliably claim that as much as 86% of the AML was being manufactured in South Africa, the main part of the remaining balance being the 4HD engine and the electromagnetic clutch. The Mk 4 arrived not long thereafter. Improvements included a more efficient fuel system and a locally manufactured electromagnetic clutch. The Mk 4 models continued in production until 1972, remaining largely unchanged except for details such as increased external stowage. By 1970, it was clear that the South African VAs had taken

on a life of their own. Although they continued to share a number of mechanical components with their French-built cousins until the introduction of the fifth mark, they also differed vastly from any Panhard production vehicle. This was no longer an exercise in badge engineering or knock-down kits, but the making of an entirely new beast. That year the VA was rebranded the Eland, and the official designation for the local equivalent of the AML 60 and AML 90 changed to Eland 60 and Eland 90 respectively.

Responding to complaints about the awkwardness of the electromagnetic clutch, which proved a challenge for the inexperienced South African crews to master and necessitated longer training times, Austral replaced that feature with a conventional pressure plate clutch for the Mk 5 series. In addition, it replaced the 1.99-litre flat-four engine with a new 2.5-litre inline 4-cylinder type, which gave noteworthy improvements in road performance. Perhaps the most significant of the Mk 5 revisions, the new engine had a reputation for being almost unbreakable. Again responding to feedback from army officials, Austral also installed new radios, an additional pintle mount on the turret roof, larger wheels and Dunlop run-flat tyres.

The Eland Mk 5 entered serial production in 1972, and a white paper published by the South African defence ministry the following year noted with approval that 98% of this mark was locally made. Ten years after Fouché's indigenisation strategy had been set into motion, production of the Eland was finally self-sufficient. In 1974, Austral, which had merged with Sandock Limited of Durban, was awarded a refurbishment contract to bring all the earlier marks still in service up to Mk 5 standards. The older models which received this upgrade were designated Mk 6 and did not differ from the Mk 5 in any significant way; they were retrofitted in successive batches when they returned from the field for routine overhaul. There were 1,016 Elands in service when the Mk 6 programme was completed.

From 1979 the Mk 6 was replaced by the Mk 7 range, which remained largely unchanged until Sandock Austral ceased production of the Eland in 1987. The Mk 7 possessed a number of novel features, including power brakes, a more robust transmission, new headlamps, and, in the Eland 90 variant, a domed cupola with vision blocks over the commander's hatch. Sandock Austral also responded to criticism levelled at the cramped crew conditions in the hull. The dimensions of the hull in the Eland Mk 7 were increased to make the driving compartment more spacious and accommodate the average size of South African armour crewmen, who were taller and larger on average than their French counterparts. Another equally important innovation was the mounting of the 2.5-litre engine on a horizontal sliding frame, allowing it to be changed in the field within 40 minutes. This was reflective of the hard lessons driven home by South African military operations in Angola, where Eland crews were expected to operate great distances from army workshops and logistical centres and carry out their own field repairs.

Production of the Mk 7 was gradually scaled back between 1976 and 1980 as Sandock Austral refocused on the development and manufacture of the Ratel infantry fighting vehicle. By 1985, the South African Army no longer had a need for such large numbers of Elands and had them increasingly relegated to second-line and reserve armour formations. Nevertheless, between 24 and 35 new Elands per month continued to be manufactured in tandem with the Ratel until production of both vehicles ceased in 1987. Production was usually between 200 and 300 Elands per year.

Between 1,300 and 1,600 Elands of all marks had been manufactured during the period 1963–87. Panhard declared in June 1994 that 1,100 AMLs had been manufactured under licence; however, the South African Defence Force (SADF) reported having 1,268 Elands in active service in 1989. This figure may not have even accounted for South Africa's entire inventory, as an unknown number of Elands were also in reserve storage or being used by the South West African Territorial Force (SWATF) auxiliary troops at the time. Many had also entered service in various export territories. It should be noted that Panhard's original licensing agreement extended only to the local assembly or production of 1,000

BELOW Soon after the AML 60 entered service with the South African Armoured Corps, the twin 7.5mm machine-guns were replaced by a single Browning M1919A4 7.62mm machine-gun. It was designated L1000 while the roof mounted Browning was the L4. This Eland 60 Mk 3 belongs to 3 Troop of E Squadron, 1st Tank Regiment.

AMLs. All Elands produced under the terms of this licence could only be re-exported with written permission from the French Minister of Defence. However, the South African and French governments reached several new arrangements concerning the licensing of military technology in January 1974, and the Panhard licence may have been renegotiated at that time. It is also unclear whether the original licensing terms could be extended to the post-1970 generation of Elands, which were produced almost wholly with South African parts and components.

The Eland can attain speeds of up to 90kmh and has an excellent road range of 450km as well as a cross-country range of 250km. It has a fuel capacity of 142 litres (31.2 Imperial gallons). The Eland's ground clearance is identical to that of the AML. It can climb a 51% gradient or 27% side slope in low gear, and ford streams to a depth of 1.1m. It may clear a trench up to 0.5m in width without sand channels, or up to 3.1m in width with the use of sand channels. Standard equipment includes the sand channels, a turret-mounted

LEFT An Eland Mk 7 kicks up the dust during a field exercise. Despite the known advantages of diesel fuel, the GM 2.5 litre petrol engine was chosen to replace the Panhard Model 4HD because of the much greater availability of petrol across South Africa.

LEFT Driver's compartment of the Eland Mk 7.

BELOW Panhard logo on rear hull.

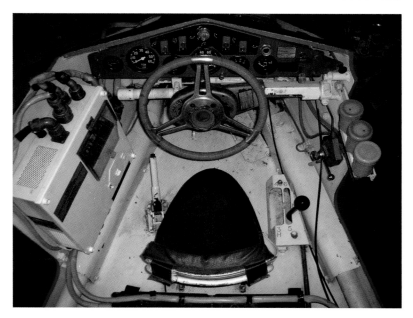

searchlight, four pneumatic bush tyres, brush guards for the driving lights, a freshwater tank, a tow bar, an external stowage box welded to the rear of the turret, and a full range of day vision equipment. Optional equipment includes night vision sights, an air conditioning and ventilation system, and the replacement of the standard petrol engine with a 2.5-litre diesel turbocharged engine.

Eland hull and turret

The Eland retains some features and an overall resemblance in common with the AML. At first glance, the most obvious shared characteristic lies in the hull, which is broadly identical in concept to that of the AML. However, the two hull types differ in size, weight and construction. The Eland's lengthier hull meant that the driving compartment was much less cramped than on the original AML. Thus more interior space was made available within the same overall wheelbase and layout. Externally, the Mk 7's hull could also be distinguished from that of its French predecessor without difficulty thanks to the relocation of both headlamps from the towing shackle to a more conventional position above the sand channels and front wheel arches. The headlamps are protected by brush guards to reduce damage from branches and other debris when navigating thick vegetation. The rear hull has also undergone a complete reconstruction, including a new engine bonnet with a ballistic grille fitted over the air intake and exhaust openings.

A stripped Eland hull bereft of any turret or equipment weighs about 4,150kg (4.1 tonnes). It is about 4m in length, 2m in width, and 1m in height. Initially the first Eland hulls were assembled using 20 sheets of prefabricated armour plate imported from France. When this material was expended, Austral found a new supplier in the South African Iron and Steel Corporation, ISCOR. Concerns about the vulnerability of the Eland were always being aired by the South African general staff, especially after experiences in the Rhodesian war proved that its hull could be penetrated by 7.62mm armour-piercing ammunition along

BELOW General Motors 2.5 litre in-line 4-cylinder water-cooled petrol engine of the Eland Mk 5, 6 and 7.

its frontal arc. During the mid-1970s, ISCOR is believed to have adopted a new technique which involved injecting a chemical mix into the steel during the refinement process, resulting in a superior type of armour plating. Thereafter all Eland hulls were manufactured with the new reinforced plate steel, which improved protection against small arms significantly.

As a result of South African operational experiences in Angola, the Eland progressively became more heavily armoured. The hull of a Mk 7 varies in thickness from 12mm to 20mm with the exception of the glacis plate, which is approximately 40mm thick. The heavier armour plate has been one of the main contributors to the increased weight of the hull. It provides the crew complete all-around protection from 7.62mm small-arms fire at any angle and shell fragments. The hull floor retains the shallow vee shape inherited from the AML, although this

offered no appreciable protection against the titanic force of the anti-tank mines South African crews routinely encountered in Angola and South West Africa. The first mine incident involving an Eland occurred in 1971, when an Eland 90 on patrol in the Caprivi Strip detonated two Soviet-built TM-46 mines. Although its hull was not penetrated, the blast itself sent the vehicle airborne and flung it about 30m away. As a result of this and other incidents, the South African Army stopped using the Eland as a point vehicle for military convoys, preferring specialised mine-protected armoured personnel carriers with much more pronounced vee-shaped hulls.

An entry door is located on each side of the hull, one opening to the front and the other opening to the rear. A fuel or water can is mounted on the exterior of the left door as standard. Above each door the hull widens into a circular flange on which the turret is bolted. The crew layout is identical to that of the AML, with the commander being seated on the left side of the turret and the gunner on the right, while the driver is seated in the hull forward of the turret. The turret is of all-welded steel construction and possesses a uniform armour thickness of 12mm. There are two smoke dischargers on either side, which are fired electrically from within the turret.

Lyttleton Engineering Works manufactured two turrets for the Eland, based on the CNMP-Berthiez HE 60-7 and H90 turrets, respectively. The South African government did not obtain a production licence to manufacture either turret until 1964, the result being that the Mk 2 and much of the Mk 3 series were assembled using surplus French turrets.

The Lyttleton variant of the HE 60-7 turret is armed with an M2 mortar on the right and a co-axial 7.62mm Browning M1919A4 machine-gun on the left. A second M1919A4 machine-gun is mounted on the turret roof for anti-aircraft defence. The M2, also identified in some sources as the Denel K1, is based on the CM60A1 and fires high-explosive, smoke and illuminating projectiles. Range and technical performance

LEFT The interior of the turret of an Eland Mark 7 shows the commander's position to the left of the 90mm gun with the gunner to its right.

are identical to the CM60A1. There are 45 mortar bombs stowed in the turret. Machine-gun ammunition is stowed in 18 boxes of 200 rounds each for a total of 3,600 7.62mm rounds. The number of mortar bombs is reduced to 35 if additional radio equipment is carried in the command role. Elands carrying this turret were designated Eland 60, or just Sixty to the troops.

A peculiar set of circumstances resulted in South African production of the H90 turret being stalled until the early 1970s. At first, the army ordered such small quantities of Eland, fitted with this turret that Sandock Austral simply filled the orders with surplus French turrets. Balanced against the army's apparent disinterest, it was cheaper to use the imported turrets rather than manufacture them locally. This changed when larger orders were placed as a result of a growing shift in strategic priorities towards the likelihood of a semi-conventional regional conflict. By 1972 Lyttleton was producing a variant of the H90 turret with a 90mm GT-2 low-recoil gun on the right and a co-axial Browning M1919A4 machine-gun on the left. South African engineers added a domed commander's cupola for this turret which has day vision blocks for 360° observation and an orientation vane sight, as well as a second M1919A4 machine-gun mounted externally on a pintle forward of the cupola. The gunner has a type M494 telescopic sight for aiming the main and secondary armament. Above the co-axial machine-gun is an extractor fan for ventilating fumes from the turret. There is sufficient stowage space to accommodate 29 main gun rounds. Machine-gun ammunition is

stowed in 11 boxes of 200 rounds each for a total of 2,200 7.62mm rounds. The GT-2 will fire any of the ammunition types developed for the DEFA D921 in addition to a South African canister round. Although the GT-2 is functionally identical to the D921, it has been fitted with a heavily modified recoil system that allows it to be fired from the turret at any angle of traverse without the risk of knocking the lightweight Eland over. Firing the gun while the Eland was in forward motion was also theoretically possible, although in practice this never occurred due to the potential for transmission damage. Elands carrying this turret were designated Eland 90.

Eland engine and chassis

The Eland's powerpack is a 2.5 litre (2,500cc) Chevrolet Motors 153 liquid-cooled 4-cylinder petrol engine. As per its name, the 153 displaces 153cu in and is rated at 67kW (90hp) at 4,000rpm. The 153 was touted for its fuel economy and compression ratio of 8.5:1, but one of the few recurring problems cited with the 4HD was the difficulty in accessing the engine or gearbox for overhaul.

Austral proposed that a new engine be fitted which could be removed from the hull and replaced by a maintenance crew with a crane in less than 90 minutes. An engine type like the 153 already in widespread circulation in the civilian market was favoured, as spare parts would be obtainable from a wide variety of sources and life cycle costs reduced accordingly. Another advantage conferred was how relatively quiet in operation the 153 proved to be. This would help the vehicle and its crew

ABOVE The combination of the 60mm mortar and co-axial Browning machine-gun continued even in the Eland Mk 7 model, although this was mainly intended for export.

LEFT A preserved Eland Mk 7 displays the insignia of Regiment Vrystaat.

BOTTOM The final model of the Eland was the Mk 7DM as supplied to Burkino Faso.

escape early detection during ambushes and deep-penetration raids into Angola.

Nowhere does the Eland owe greater allegiance to its AML predecessor than in the integral features of its articulated suspension and drive system, which have survived all seven marks virtually unchanged. Drive is transmitted through a single-plate clutch that is hydraulically operated, eliminating the AML's intricate and overly complex electromagnetic clutch. The clutch conveys drive to the same transversely mounted gearbox with six forward and one reverse gear incorporating the patented Panhard slip differential. From the gearbox drive is conveyed to two lateral transfer boxes, and then by pinions to the rear wheel stations and by drive shafts to the front wheel stations. From the wheel bevel gears it reaches the epicyclic gearing in the hub after being conveyed through a train of gears housed within cast trailing arms, upon which the wheels are mounted. The Eland still possesses the same independent suspension system – composed of coil springs and oil-damped shock-absorbers acting on the trailing arms – it inherited from the AML.

The brakes are vacuum assisted, with internal expanding shoes on all four wheels. The wheels are of the split rim type and are fitted with Dunlop 12.00 x 16-Trak Grip tyres. The tyres possess reinforced sidewalls and run-flat inserts to resist puncture from enemy fire as well as the abrasive effects of fallen limbs, tree stumps, thorny vegetation and other environmental detritus in the African bush. The larger and wider tyres increased ground clearance and therefore cross-country mobility over all types of terrain. There were seven different types of Eland culminating in the Mk 7, to which standard almost all earlier models were subsequently refurbished.

OPPOSITE Three-view drawing of Panhard AML 90.

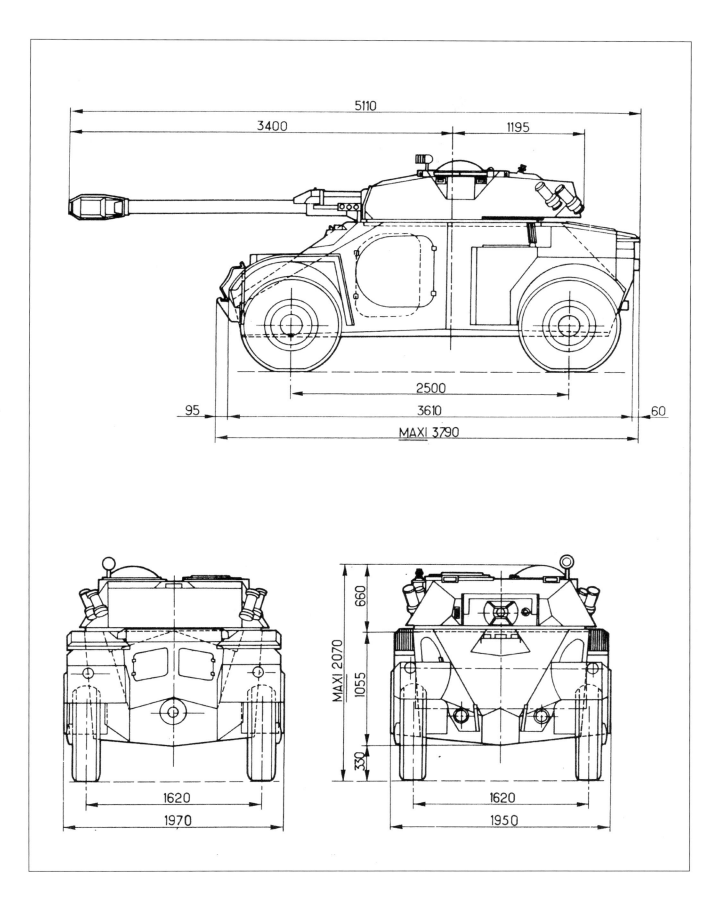

Chapter Four

AML
variants

There are few AFV designs that have generated so many derivatives and variants as the Panhard AML and its M3 VTT Armoured Personnel Carrier companion. Such a diversity of applications, from anti-tank guided weapons to anti-aircraft gun versions and from mortar carriers to armoured ambulances, creates a complete family of vehicles to meet a whole host of tactical requirements on the battlefield with the advantage of logistical commonality.

OPPOSITE The most sophisticated anti-aircraft variant of the Panhard AML series is the TTB 120 RT VDA incorporating considerable firepower for such a compact vehicle.

There is no question that the basic soundness of the AML and VTT designs allowed a whole host of versatile variants to be created on the basic chassis of the two vehicles. It is a measure of the strength of the French arms industry that quite so many have been produced, although many of these projects did not proceed beyond the prototype stage. Nevertheless, each and every one of them was viable within the context of the time and advanced the design and development of subsequent AFVs. In consequence, France remains one of the market leaders in the production of armoured cars across the world with a whole host of wheeled vehicles to meet the requirements of any armed forces.

ABOVE The standard production AML 60 was equipped with a 60mm HB 60CM-A1 mortar with twin 7.62 ANF1 machine-guns (originally with twin 7.5mm AA-52). The Hotchkiss-Brandt HB 60CM-A1 fires standard HB 60mm mortar ammunition types and can also fire special anti-tank rounds with a maximum range of 500m in direct-fire mode. Vehicle weight is 4.8 tonnes.

OPPOSITE The original H60 turret is armed with twin machine-guns and a single 60mm mortar. The machine-guns can be elevated from −15 to +60° and the mortar from −15 to +80°. The TDA Model HB 60 can be used in the direct role up to a range of 500m or in the indirect role up to a range of 2,600m. In the basic model, 53 mortar bombs and 3,800 rounds of 7.62mm machine-gun ammunition are carried; if additional radios are installed for the command role, ammunition is reduced to 32 mortar bombs and 3,200 rounds of machine-gun ammunition. Types of mortar bomb include HE, canister, smoke and illuminating. The turret is provided with a large two-piece hatch cover that opens to the front and rear of the vehicle, seven periscopes (Model L794B) and an M112/M113 periscope with a magnification of x5 for aiming.

LEFT This is almost identical to the HE 60-7 turret but is armed with a 12.7mm (0.50in) machine-gun and a TDA 60mm HB 60 mortar. The machine-gun can be elevated from −15 to +60° and the mortar from −15 to +80°. A total of 43 mortar bombs and 1,300 rounds of 12.7mm machine-gun ammunition is carried. If additional radios are carried, ammunition load is reduced to 31 rounds of 60mm and 900 rounds of 12.7mm machine-gun ammunition. Loaded weight of an AML with the HE 60-12 turret is 4,800kg.

AML H90

LEFT The H90 turret is manufactured by Hispano-Suiza and armed with a Giat Industries 90mm D 921 F1 gun which fires **HEAT, HE,** smoke and canister rounds. A 7.62mm coaxial machine-gun is mounted to the left of the main armament. The two smoke grenade dischargers mounted on each side of the turret are electrically fired from within the vehicle. Vehicle weight is 5.5 tons with a three-man crew. The CN-90-F1 was one of the most important Cold War gunnery developments conducted by **DEFA** and its successor **DTAT.** The gun was developed from 1955 by the Section Technique d'Artillerie (ST/ART) at Saint-Cloud as the D921A, a weapon envisaged to be fired from light armoured vehicles in the 5- to 6-tonne range. The intended mounting was expected to be the Engin Léger de Combat, a two-man 6-tonne light AFV with a turreted 90mm low-pressure gun. Recoil forces were kept to a manageable level (about 3,500kg) by the choice of lightweight, low-velocity ammunition that depended on chemical energy projectiles for armour penetration (Hollow Charge Heat Rounds), stabilised in flight by integral fins housed in the cartridge case prior to firing, forming a sort of tail that stabilised the round in flight. The round was known as the 90-ARE (ARE being the abbreviation given to the Atelier de Roanne, but was also the first three letters of the engineer in charge of the hollow charge round project's name, Ingénieur en Chef Arene). The aluminium-shelled 90mm HEAT round was adopted in 1961 as the Obus a Charge Creuse Empenné 90mm Mle 62 or OCC-90-62. The D921A gun could fire the OCC-90-62 to an effective range of 1,000m. A welded muzzle brake based on the experience of the development of the M51 Sherman's 105mm gun for Israel was employed on D921A to further reduce recoil shock.

RIGHT In 1970, 1st Special Service Battalion at Zeerust produced an 'Eland Gun Truck' as a convoy escort vehicle for operations in South West Africa and Angola. Despite interest from the General Staff, it was not adopted for service despite the widespread use of such vehicles in Vietnam at the time.

AML LYNX 90

RIGHT The AML Lynx 90 has been purchased by Burundi and Morocco and 23 were given to the Chadian National Armed Forces as military aid during the war with Libya. Similarly small numbers were given to Guinea, Senegal and Togo by the French government. The Lynx turret is also offered as part of an upgrade package for existing AMLs that has been adopted by Lebanon and Kenya in its ongoing conflict with Al-Shabab.

A M L 90 F1 - LYNX - DIESEL

BELOW The AML Lynx 90 is the modernised version of the AML H90 mounting the same armament, but the Lynx turret can be fitted with a greater variety of fire control equipment such as a laser rangefinder and night vision devices. The Lynx 90 turret also offers powered traverse and elevation in place of the former manual controls. Similar in configuration to the Eland, the commander has a raised rotating cupola for all-round observation. As before, a white light spotlight is mounted coaxially with the 90mm D921 gun that now fires APFSDS ammunition. This can be combined with the same Canasta night sights and fire control system as the AMX-10RC. An alternative main armament is the more powerful Cockerill Mk III medium-pressure 90mm gun. A host of optional extras are available for the vehicle to allow customers to configure the AML Lynx 90 to their particular specification.

M3 VTT (VÉHICULE DE TRANSPORT DE TROUPES)

LEFT The M3 VTT or Véhicule de Transport de Troupes (Armoured Personnel Carrier) was developed from the AML 245 using the same mechanical components as the AML series with a commonality of 95%. Panhard designed the VTT as a private venture in 1967. Although it did not see service with the French Army, the VTT was sold in large numbers to foreign armies. It is crewed by a vehicle commander and driver and can carry ten men or 3,000lb of cargo. The all-welded steel armour of 0.31in to 0.47in (8mm to 12mm) thickness gives adequate armour protection against small arms and artillery fragments while the V-profile floor improves survivability against attack by land mines. It can be configured in command, recovery, communications, cargo and ambulance versions. It can be equipped with cupola mounted weapon systems or with a range of powered turrets including single and twin 20mm cannon mountings as well as a range of Anti-Tank Guided Weapon (ATGW) systems.

CENTRE AND LEFT The prototype Panhard M3 VTT first appeared in August 1969 and development testing continued until 1971. The vehicle incorporated a box-like superstructure of 10 to 12mm welded steel armour giving protection against small-arms fire and artillery fragments. Such a configuration allowed the vehicle to be amphibious without further preparation. It featured a Creusot-Loire CAFL-38S turret armed with the standard French 7.5mm AA-52 machine-gun that was originally mounted on the AMX VCI. Access to the troop compartment was via a large door on each side and twin doors at the rear. With a combat weight of 12,760lb as against 10,560lb for the AML H60, the VTT was somewhat underpowered with the same Panhard 4HD 97bhp engine.

RIGHT Series production of the Panhard M3 VTT began in April 1971. The vehicle now featured a redesigned hull incorporating three firing hatches on each side with two more in the rear doors. The simplest weapon option was a Creusot-Loire STB Rotary Support Shield suitable for the French AA-52 machine-gun as the STB 52 (shown here); the STB 80 for the Belgian MAG 80; STB MG for the West German MG3 and the STB 30 for the 7.6 mm Browning. The driver is situated in the front hull just to the left of the centreline. Behind him is the engine in an enclosed compartment but its position is a cause of discomfort to the crew and dismounts. A total of 1,180 M3 VTT and variants was produced up until 1986 at a unit cost of $166,000 for the basic vehicle in that year.

ABOVE LEFT AND ABOVE AML Internal Security. The configuration of the M3 VTT is well suited for Internal Security or IS duties with space for up to ten riot police. The vehicle is fitted with both non-lethal weapons such as the grenade launchers to the rear firing pepper spray or CS gas canisters or else a machine-gun at the commander's hatch. This version has been purchased by undisclosed countries in the Gulf States.

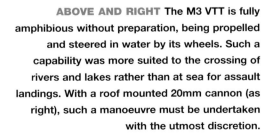

ABOVE AND RIGHT The M3 VTT is fully amphibious without preparation, being propelled and steered in water by its wheels. Such a capability was more suited to the crossing of rivers and lakes rather than at sea for assault landings. With a roof mounted 20mm cannon (as right), such a manoeuvre must be undertaken with the utmost discretion.

M3 TOUCAN 1

ABOVE LEFT This M3 features a GIAT Toucan 1 cupola mounting an M693 20mm dual-feed or M621 single-feed cannon with an elevation of +50° and depression of –13° for maximum flexibility against aircraft or ground targets, especially in urban areas. The 20mm cannon incorporates a coaxial 7.62mm machine-gun and spotlight. This weapon installation was just one offered by French manufacturers to arm the M3 VTT and associated light AFVs.

ABOVE An advertisement from Creusot-Loire illustrates the number of armament options available for the M3 VTT and like vehicles. Similar turrets and mountings were offered by a range of French manufacturers to meet any requirement.

VAT (VÉHICULE ATELIER TRANSPORT)

CENTRE AND LEFT The VAT was designed to undertake recovery and repair of AML family vehicles in the combat zone. Extensive repair equipment is carried including a generator, specialised tools, inspection lamps, tow bars and cables as well as welding gear. A penthouse can be erected at the rear to allow repairs to be carried out under cover at night or in bad weather. A block and tackle can be fitted above the roof to enable engines and other vehicle components to be exchanged. The VAT was in service with several armies equipped with the AML and M3 VTT series.

VPC (VÉHICULE POSTE DE COMMANDE)

Command version of the M3, with an armoured body with a front troop compartment sitting up to five men. The rear part of the body is a communications compartment with four 180AH batteries and two wireless operators' positions. The VPC can mount the following radio systems: Short range: ANVRC10, TRVP213, TRVP11, RT524. Communication to regiment level: ANGRC9, TRVP213-BLU, TRC432, TRC372, TRC310, TRC320, VRC12, VRC53, ANVRO3. Air liaison: UHF 30-35, RF301 (238–248MHz) on pre-regulated frequencies, TRAP35, teletype sets (BLU). Six antennae bases are provided as standard.

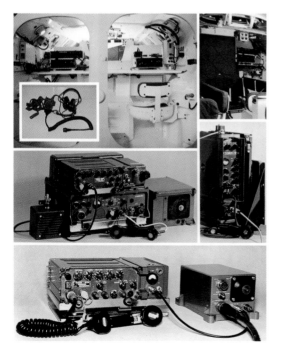

The M3 VTS is configured to carry four stretchers or six sitting wounded or four sitting wounded and two stretchers. It is crewed by a driver and two medical orderlies. The rear access doors of the M3 hull are enlarged for easy access for standard stretchers. An air conditioning system is among the options listed for the VTS. Displaying prominent Red Crescent markings, this M3 VTS is in service with the Bahrain Defence Force. The latter procured a total of 133 AML and M3 variants with the ATS being the last in service. *(Dick Taylor)*

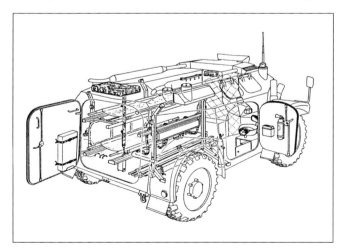

PANHARD M3 VLA ENGINEER VEHICLE

Panhard M3 APC fitted with a hydraulically operated 2.2m-wide dozer blade at the front of the hull that is used for clearing obstacles and filling in craters etc. The crew comprises the commander and driver of the vehicle together with a four-man pioneer section and their specialised tools in the rear. The vehicle is armed with a Creusot-Loire STB rotary support shield with a 7.62mm machine-gun that is fired by the commander.

AML AMPHIBIE

To enhance its tactical mobility, the basic models of the AML series can be fitted with floatation equipment to allow them to negotiate rivers and waterways with the minimum of preparation. This is an AML HS-30. One of the design criteria for the original AML was that the vehicle was to be amphibious but this requirement compromised the basic design to an unacceptable degree.

The Panhard HS 30 is equipped with a 30mm Type 831 cannon in a Hispano-Suiza turret with an elevation of up to +45° to engage low-flying aircraft and an all-round traverse of 360° in 20 seconds. The vehicle carries 200 rounds of 30mm ammunition and 2,200 of 7.62mm. The cannon can be fired at a high rate of 650 rounds a minute for aerial targets and a low rate as well as single shot against ground targets. This variant was presented at the Sartory Arms Exhibition in 1971 but did not proceed beyond the prototype stage.

AML 40

Introduced in 1990, the AML 40 is a Panhard AML 60-7 with the turret modified to accept a 7.62mm machine-gun and the Spanish Santa Barbara 40mm automatic grenade launcher with a maximum range of 2,200m; it has a cyclic rate of fire of 200 rounds/min and a muzzle velocity of 240m/sec with a total of 225 rounds of 40mm and 1,250 rounds of 7.62mm ammunition carried.

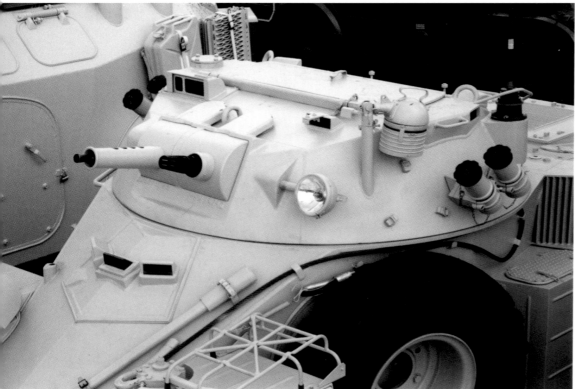

PANHARD M3 THOMSON-BRANDT MORTIER 120MM

ABOVE Panhard M3 towing a Thomson-Brandt Mortier 120mm Rayé Tracté Modele F1 or '120mm rifled towed mortar model F1' whereby the weapon is towed by a hitch screwed into the muzzle with the M3 VTM or Véhicule Tracteur Mortier de 120mm acting as the prime mover. The latter carries up to 70 mortar bombs and the crew of four gunners as well as the vehicle driver and commander. The mortar has a rate of fire of six to ten rounds/min with an effective range of 8,200m when firing the 18.7kg PR-14 HE bomb with a kill radius of 75m.

AML S530 AA 20MM

RIGHT In 1971, Panhard produced specifically for export an anti-aircraft variant of the AML in cooperation with the Société d'Applications des Machines Motrices (SAMM) featuring an S 530 turret armed with twin M621 20mm cannons. The latter have an elevation of +75 degrees and depression of −10 degrees with 260 rounds/barrel that can be fired as single shots, in short bursts or fully automatic at a cyclic rate of 740 rounds/min/barrel with the empty cartridge cases ejected externally. The S530 turret incorporates optical ranging via a roof mounted periscopic sight. This version was purchased by Venezuela and 12 were produced and delivered by 1973.

VDA (VÉHICULE DÉFENSE ANTI-AÉRIENNE)

In 1972, development began on a new self-propelled anti-aircraft gun system based on the M3 VTT under the designation Véhicule de Défense Anti-aérienne or VDA. The vehicle was a joint development between Panhard and Electronique Serge Dassault with major subcontractors of Hispano-Suiza for the turret, Oerlikon for the guns and Gallileo for the sights. The first VDA prototype was completed in December 1973 and production began in April 1975. The main armament comprises two Hispano-Suiza 820 SL 20mm cannons mounted externally on the one-man TA20 turret housing the gunner. The latter has the choice of firing single shots, bursts or on fully automatic at a cyclic rate of 200 or 1,000 rounds/barrel/min. The higher rate of fire is only possible with the four outriggers deployed to provide stability. The weapons have a maximum elevation of +85º and depression of –5º with a turret traverse of 360º. Mounted at the rear of the turret is an ESD RA-20 pulse-Doppler radar for both surveillance and target acquisition with the capacity to track four targets simultaneously. The maximum effective range of the 20mm cannon is 1,500m at altitude and 2,500m horizontally. Each barrel is provided with 300 rounds of ready use ammunition including high explosive incendiary and armour piercing. The VDA has seen service with the Ivory Coast, Niger and the United Arab Emirates.

AML SAMM 120 VDA

RIGHT A later anti-aircraft variant of the Véhicule Défense Anti-aérienne based on the AML chassis is the SAMM 120 20mm two-man turret. Of all welded steel construction, the turret is divided into two separate sealed compartments with the 20mm armament in the front with the crew and all the systems controls in the rear. The main armament comprises a 20mm M693(F2) dual-feed cannon with 140 rounds of HE and 80 of AP with a maximum elevation of +50° and depression of −8° as shown above. Coaxial armament is a standard 7.62mm machine-gun.

BELOW The variants of the AML 245 have come full circle with the introduction of the EPR Scout Car that has a very similar configuration to the original Ferret Mk 1 employed during the War in Algeria and afterwards. The EPR is a standard AML without a turret and armed with a ring-mounted .5-calibre M2 HB machine-gun. Powered by a Peugeot XD 3T 95bhp diesel engine, the EPR comes in various versions including the ERA armed raiding vehicle for Special Forces; the EPF border protection vehicle and the EPA airfield defence vehicle.

AML NA2

This vehicle was developed by Nord-Aviation, hence NA, in conjunction with Panhard to create a long-range anti-tank variant of the AML given the range limitations of the low-recoil 90mm DEFA gun. The NA2 turret can carry and launch four SS-11 or two SS-12 anti-tank guided missiles (ATGM). The designation 'SS' denotes sol-à-sol, or surface-to-surface. The SS-11 entered service with the French Army in 1956 whereas AS-11 was the air-launched version that was first used in combat during the Algerian War leading to the introduction of ATGM-armed combat helicopters. As a MGLOS (Manually Guided Line-of-Sight) missile, the SS-11 has an effective range of 500 to 3,000m with the capacity to destroy all contemporary battle tanks. The AML NA2 did not enter production but a later version of the SS-11, designated Harpon with a much simplified guidance system, was fitted to the turret of the AML, be it H90 or H60, as here.

VTT TH TOURELLE HOT

This is the M3 VTT fitted with the Euromissile UTM 800 HOT (Haut subsonique Optiquement Téléguidé Tiré d'un Tube, or High Subsonic Optical Remote-Guided, Tube-Launched) turret mounted on a raised plinth above the vehicle. The turret has four ready to launch 4,000m range HOT missiles and another ten missiles carried in reserve in the hull that are loaded via a hatch in the right rear of the roof. The turret has an optical sight

with a magnification of ×3 (18° field of view) and ×12 (5° field of view), elevation being +22°, depression −10° and turret traverse 360°. The HOT ATGW has an armour penetration capability of 1,250mm. The HOT missile system has been sold to almost 20 countries but primarily in the helicopter-launched role.

The rear door of the VTT TH is a single-piece hatch to allow easier loading and stowage for the supplementary ten HOT ATGW.

AML SERVAL

ABOVE Panhard AML with HE 60-20 Serval Hispano-Suiza CNMP turret displaying the variety of weapons including the 60mm HB Longue Portée mortar and M693 20mm cannon with its coaxial 7.62mm machine-gun. The vehicle can be configured with a range of options including an NBC system, laser rangefinder and a power-assisted turret traverse mechanism with a 360° rate of 7.5sec.

BELOW A Panhard AML HE 60-20 Serval leads a pair of AML 60-7s and AML 90s during a military parade of the Niger Armed Forces. As one of the ultimate variants of the AML 245 series, the Serval turret can be offered as part of an upgrade package together with the Peugeot XD 3T 95bhp diesel engine.

M3 BUFFALO

A Panhard Buffalo is shown in the white colour scheme of the United Nations peacekeeping forces before delivery to a foreign customer, with Rwanda employing the vehicle as part of UNMISS (United Nations Mission in South Sudan) in Sudan's Western Darfur region in 2005.

The development of a successor to the M3 VTT began in 1983 specifically for the export market. The vehicle is called the Buffalo and bears a striking resemblance to its predecessor. The Buffalo was introduced in June 1985 and production was undertaken on 'an as needed' basis. Among the many enhancements are the external stowage boxes over the wheel arches that absorb and detach when subjected to mine attack, so preserving the integrity of the hull. The vehicle comes with either a spark or compression ignition Peugeot engine. As with the M3, the Buffalo comes in several versions including command, 81mm mortar carrier, engineer and maintenance vehicles as well as ambulance. Among the options available is a front mounted winch as shown here and air conditioning. While the basic APC variant is armed with a .50-calibre machine-gun,

other weapons and enclosed turrets can be fitted to the vehicle. The Panhard Buffalo has not enjoyed the sales success of the M3 VTT with just 142 purchased as against 1,180. Customers include Benin, Colombia, Rwanda and Tunisia.

AML JUNGLE

ABOVE This vehicle is a version of the AML scout car and is fitted with a SAMM BTM one-man turret mounting 12.7mm and 7.62mm machine-guns as well as nine grenade launchers to allow a swift withdrawal behind a wall of smoke or to engage close-range troops with canister fire. A total of 1,000 rounds of 12.7mm and 2,300 7.62mm ammunition are stowed in the vehicle. It is powered by the Peugeot XD 3T diesel engine producing 95hp coupled to the standard Panhard transmission.

AML ÉCLAIRAGE

LEFT Unveiled at the Eurosatory ground defence exhibition in 1983, the AML scout car model features a new two-man turret from Panhard. The turret is an open design and is fitted with an M693 20mm cannon and a 7.62mm machine-gun coaxially mounted. A total of 1,050 rounds of 20mm ammunition and 2,000 rounds of 7.62mm ammunition is carried. The weapons can be elevated +45° and depressed −8° and the turret can be traversed 360°. This model, powered by the Peugeot XD 3T diesel, can be optionally fitted with a Euromissile MILAN (Missile d´Infanterie Léger Antichar) anti-tank guided missile system.

AML UPGRADES

Despite being in service for over 50 years there is still a thriving business in refurbishment and upgrading of all members of the AML family. In France, SOFEMA (Société Française d'Exportation de Matériel Militaire et Aéronautique) holds the AML brand and patents from Panhard and is still active in the acquisition, overhaul, product improvement and selling of AML armoured cars across the world. In Belgium, Sabiex SA International provided a similar service for the AML 90 and 60 as did Saymar Ltd in Israel. The primary improvement is the replacement of the Panhard 95bhp petrol engine with a more fuel efficient diesel unit. Other sub-systems upgraded include the manual transmission, new engine cooling system, new and improved electrical system, new disc braking system all round, hydraulic powered steering, new turret electrical system, communications and intercom system. All new electrical components include more reliable electrical wire bundles, electric voltage regulator, 24v 65amp generator, 24v starter, new driver's panel and new instrument panel. This upgrade can be carried out in the user's own facilities with the aid of kits provided by SOFEMA, or the company can carry out the work in its own facilities in Châteauroux. This upgrade package can also be combined with a general overhaul of the vehicle to bring it up to an almost new-build standard.

ABOVE LEFT SOFEMA offers an upgraded model designated the AML-90F1 Génération Nouvelle incorporating thermal imaging, an integrated laser rangefinder and a host of other improvements. *(Steven Zaloga)*

LEFT Another variant of the basic modernised Panhard hull is the AML Pégase that is armed with a single 12.7mm heavy machine-gun. It is intended for convoy escort and peacekeeping operations as its white livery suggests. *(Steven Zaloga)*

Chapter Five

AML restoration

It is gratifying to note that the restoration of historical AFVs is now widespread across the world. Intriguingly, there are few Panhard AMLs in private hands since any usable vehicle is snapped up by SOFEMA to be refurbished and resold on the international arms market. Barrimore England-Davis has two superb examples of an AML 60 and 90 that he has painstakingly restored to their former glory.

OPPOSITE At a scrapyard in northern France a discarded AML awaits the scrap man's blow torch.

Locating

Allow me to quote a well-known saying: you wait ages for a bus then three come along at once. I had watched Panhard AMLs enter the collectors' market (and leave again) for a number of years. After preparing a restoration space in my workshop and purchasing an HGV for transportation I decided to take the plunge, but I couldn't find any. Typical, I thought, that well-known saying just wasn't playing out when I wanted it to.

I started my search for an AML by visiting some private collections of military vehicles in France, where I used 'fixers' to get me the introductions. Unfortunately nearly all of the AMLs that I found had been demilitarised quite thoroughly by cutting the hull in half, or were available 'without paperwork'. Anyone who's ever tried exporting armoured vehicles from France without the proper paperwork will know it simply won't happen – so I started looking in other countries that had also used the Panhard AML.

Eventually I found a rich 'seam' of Panhards advertised in Spain. The Spanish had bought a good number from the French and these vehicles had reached the end of their useful lives in the late 1970s or early '80s. As a result there were a number still in use as gate guardians, as commemorative edifices, or simply sitting in scrapyards rotting away. The examples offered to me in Spain all proved to be incomplete and were missing major components such as the interiors, engines or

gearboxes. I decided this probably wasn't a good basis for a restoration as I had no idea about parts availability. What I wanted was a complete vehicle.

I tried a revised approach by actively generating my own lead on a complete vehicle. I placed a 'wanted' advert in a classic car magazine published in Spain and Portugal. Using a 99p supermarket mobile phone sim card I recorded any inbound calls generated by the ads as I couldn't speak to anyone – I wasn't fluent in Spanish or Portuguese. With liberal quantities of red wine I convinced my Spanish-speaking friend to scan any messages left on the mobile number, jot down any leads, and we could go from there. This actually worked very well and a few useful messages were left for me.

I ended up travelling to Spain twice, chasing up leads that were brought about by my advert. Following up the second phone call, I came across an AML that was at least 80% complete. This turned out to be quite an achievement as there seemed a tendency to cannibalise any non-restored vehicles to keep other examples on the road – but I had managed to find one. Although rusty and bashed about it had all the parts I needed to start off a decent restoration.

The owner only wanted 100 Euros and I think he was glad it was finally going to be restored. He had started the restoration in the '90s but stopped when he realised Spanish law prohibited the driving of armoured vehicles by private individuals.

I took my newly acquired (but ancient) recovery lorry on the freight ferry from Plymouth to Bilbao and drove to his location on the Portuguese border. I loaded the vehicle, set off after a fantastic lunch with the chap and his family, accidentally clipped his driveway gates on the way out, and set off home very pleased with the deal. The truck only broke down once on the way back – possibly a miracle with such an exhausted lorry.

Back at my workshop in the UK I examined the AML and it became clear it had originally been used by the Spanish Marines, which was apparent from the markings on the hull and turret. I had also gleaned some of its history from the previous owner. After its naval use the vehicle had languished as a public exhibit outside the Marines base in Pontevedra. After being extensively vandalised and covered in teenagers' graffiti it was removed from display because it was getting 'dangerous' and eventually ended up in a local scrapyard. The owner, knowing the vehicle had disappeared, tracked it down to the scrapyard and rescued it. And so the vehicle was deposited in my workshop and the strip-down began.

I attacked the restoration with vigour, but it was very hard-going. I didn't really have a blueprint of how things went together so it was rather like having a 3D jigsaw puzzle, but with no idea of the picture on the box lid. Fortunately for me, part-way through this restoration another two AMLs surfaced in a scrapyard, this

ABOVE AND LEFT A privately owned AML in northern Spain; and the vehicle just after I took ownership is loaded on to the transport for recovery to the UK.

ABOVE A Gendarmerie AML awaits destruction at a scrapyard in northern France in January 2013.

vehicles. When the initial AML 60 was complete, I acted on a tip-off from another contact I had made in the French military vehicle scene, and secured another three! The buses were finally turning up! This time the vehicles were complete examples from France. It appears they had been auctioned off in the early '90s and had come from a reserve stock. They had just been sitting outside ever since (unfortunately with their turret hatches open) awaiting a new owner.

I managed to organise an export licence at great cost and had the AMLs delivered to me, only this time by a haulier. Unfortunately they were transported in a curtain-side lorry and hadn't been tied down correctly. When they arrived they were battered where they'd shunted into each other repeatedly on the back of the truck, and then we had quite a job trying to unload them with no ramps. The driver expected me to fork-lift them out of his lorry (no easy task at 4.5 tons each) so I felt he hadn't really understood that these were armoured cars and not just some sort of heavy pallet.

The three AMLs entered my restoration unit and I set about working on them, applying all the lessons I had learned to date. When these were completed I retained one and the others were passed to museums.

Once the dust had settled I had thought

time in France. Following a tip-off from a French contact, I managed to strike a deal with the yard owner and I was given a small window of opportunity to strip what I could off the hulls. The work took place over two very cold days in an ice-bound scrapyard where the thermometer never rose above −2°. After I had finished with the vehicles, what was left was then thoroughly demilitarised (smashed unfortunately) by the yard owner and then melted down.

To complete the restoration of the Spanish AML 60 I had to utilise parts from all three

RIGHT Three mothballed AMLs 'saved' from France and returned to the UK for restoration.

I had satisfied my AML 'itch' with these adventures, but I started to harbour designs on trying to restore an AML 90.

One evening I was idly browsing the internet to try and find out what had happened to the exhibits once displayed at the defunct Army Transport Museum in Beverley, Yorkshire. While doing so I came across a review on Trip Advisor of a Napoleonic military fort at the edge of the Humber estuary, Fort Paull. This review included some pictures, and there in one of the snaps, to my great surprise, was a rather sad-looking and decomposing AML 90.

After a few weeks' negotiations with the museum's extremely helpful owner and enthusiastic staff an exchange was organised – two French Army soft-skins in exchange for the sad-looking wreck of the AML 90.

Work started once again on a Panhard, but this AML had suffered terribly from being left open to the elements for 20 years near the estuary. It had a chequered history that included being used as a German armoured car in films, and being eventually set alight while filming the finale of the modern-day version of Shakespeare's *Richard III* in 1995. It now had a nest of rats living in the gun barrel and at least two trees growing out of the engine bay.

Back at the workshop I removed what I could. After digging out half a foot of debris from inside the hull and a lot of dead wildlife, the picture wasn't looking too favourable for the 'old soldier'. Nearly everything that could

rust away had. In fact, damage to the AML 90 was so severe that I had to replace nearly everything I legitimately could, using items from the large inventory of spares I had built up. One of the greatest challenges involved the main gun, which was stuck at full recoil. I needed to cut open the mantle to free up the main armament. After a great deal of blood, sweat and many tears the vehicle is now complete, fully roadworthy, UK-registered and ready for display.

Restoration of Panhard AMLs in detail

The AML 60 and 90 share the same hull design, except for a few small details, so the following restoration guide is based on a generic hull reconstruction and looks at both turrets individually.

Bodywork

The construction of the hull is a basic welded rhomboid shape, with wheels on each corner attached to wheel stations that contain the portal drives to the wheels. The front wheel stations are finished off with large oversize front wings. The rear of the vehicle has two large stowage boxes on each side and the exhaust/ air intake tray. This constitutes the simple rear wing, mounted above the rear wheel station. It all bolts together rather like a large 'Meccano' kit.

ABOVE A Panhard AML 90 'discovered' on Trip Advisor at Fort Paull in the north of England. The vehicle was dragged from its resting place ready for transportation.

ABOVE AND LEFT The same AML 90 after strip-down (above); the wings and stowage bins (left) were beyond repair.

As such, the body work is comparatively straightforward to refurbish or indeed replace. The rear wings and stowage boxes are almost square and single-skinned, so they are easy to refabricate or patch where necessary, from inside and out. The front wings are a good deal harder to refurbish as they have compound curves and the restorer will need a modicum of panel beating experience. That said, this is no more difficult than working on a modern or classic car body, as the wings can be easily taken off the hull and worked on with basic tools and little need for any finesse.

If the wings are missing completely this can be a little more challenging. With no panels to start with, you are left guessing what they should look like as well as the dimensions. If you choose to engage a professional refabricator, a good deal of time is likely to be spent on construction drawings and then in the manufacture. This can become costly and, after my early investigation, I discovered the cost of having a wing made from scratch could be more than £1,000.

I was in a very fortunate position to have spare wings, which I had sourced from a scrapyard in France. Therefore, in my case it was just a case or taking off the old and bolting on the new. This is very straightforward and uses simple metric nuts and bolts. There were a few patches of rust to address, but this was achieved with simple, flat, mild steel hammered into shape.

The hull is manufactured from hardened nickel steel so it does not rust readily. Indeed, the welds that hold the hull together can clean up to appear as if they were welded only yesterday. To restore the exterior of the hull was simply a case of flattening back the multitude of layers of military-grade paint, then priming and respraying.

However, the difficulties lie within the hull. The hull is watertight up to the bottom of the door openings, and these are about 4in from the lowest point of the floor. Therefore, any water ingress that is not drained out can sit in the bottom of the hull and start to rust away at components. The bungs in the hull bottom can rust in-situ and then draining is near impossible. The hull floor can start to rust, forming a number of horris 'scabs', but it is the mounting points for the driver's seat, fuel tank, drive shafts, gear change lever and footbrake that will suffer the most. At the very least these mounting points will probably need a good clean, but if their integrity is compromised they will need replacing. Welding armour is an art because the heat from the weld dissipates extremely quickly, so it is a good idea to heat up the area first before commencing a weld, or utilise a very high welding setting (either gas or electrical).

Painting

Once the vehicle body is reassembled it is best to seal the old military-grade paint externally. I used a few coats of sealer, then a two-pack primer and finished off with a colour-matched cellulose or two-pack top coat. I found using a satin top coat seems to work best as it partially reflects the light and gives a crisp finish to the exterior. Using the satin is not a million miles away from the satin-finished paints used by the French armed forces throughout the 1960s. The interior will see a lot of traffic, therefore I use a readily available white 'metal paint' that can be thinned and sprayed, or applied directly with a brush. Don't be afraid of painting the outside of the vehicle with a good quality brush

ABOVE AND BELOW Front right wing detail showing a good dose of tin worm (above) and the same wing after repaired sections had been welded in.

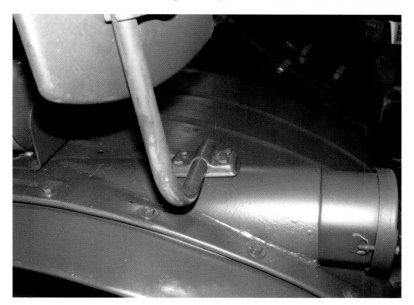

or even use a small roller if you don't have the facilities to spray paint. With a good quality tool, and the paint thinned, a very good finish can be achieved. It will just take a lot longer and you'll need to constantly be on the look-out for paint runs.

Vehicle markings

Once the paintwork is finished it's time for decals. Some restorers prefer hand-painting theirs, but I have a stock of high-quality scans of original decals, so I had these reproduced and printed on self-adhesive vinyl. If you're unsure your decals are the ones you'll want to keep in the long term, you can source vinyl decals that have been mounted on a magnetic backing so they can be stuck to the hull and then taken off again easily. The font for the number plate is described as 'European number plate' by the graphic design shops, but I was able to touch up the originals, using silver satin cellulose on a matt black background.

There is always a dilemma when you uncover lots of markings, deciding upon which unit, country or registration you should use. I was spoiled for choice as the AML 90 had three number plates, painted one on top of the other, illustrating how the vehicle had been recycled with different nations over the years. I decided to strip back to the original French number and ignore the two Israeli numbers on top.

Electrics

External lighting is quite straightforward. The vehicle is 24v so it utilises a lot of lamps and spotlights as found on most French military vehicles from the 1950s to the '90s. Sidelights are straightforward and can be purchased from new old stock – they are the same as on the Willys and Hotchkiss Jeeps. The more tricky items to source were the searchlights. With years on public display, some vehicles attract 'magpies' and so these lighting units can disappear easily. However, they come up for

BELOW Modern 12v batteries connected in series in the battery location behind the driver.

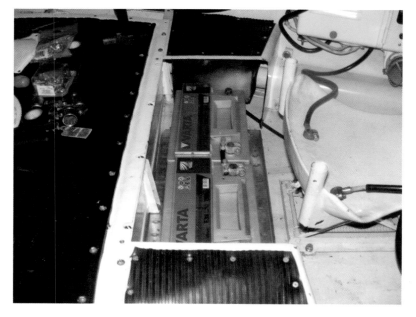

sale surprisingly regularly when the 'magpies' are bored with their finds and want to turn them into cash.

Interestingly, the electrics on the engine are also quite generic and shared across a number of French soft-skin vehicles (eg the Hotchkiss M201 Jeep), so getting HT leads, the dizzy and coil is not an issue as there are lots of such items in the UK and France.

The dials and switch gear are also shared with French military soft-skins, so a Simca lorry dash 'box' was purchased and nearly everything needed was lifted and transplanted into the Panhard from this.

The one specialised item not shared with any other vehicle is the fuse box/panel. This installation sits to the left of the driver and contains all the fuses, light controls and, most importantly, the regulator. It's the one item you want to make sure you have available and serviceable before you start a restoration. If you try to rewire the box, it soon becomes very complex as there is a tangle of spaghetti-like wires that all seem to be the same white colour! The fuse box contains circuit-breakers, so there's no need to replace fuses every time you wire something up incorrectly on your rebuild – you simply press the reset buttons!

There are two interior lights in the turrets of both vehicles. These are very simple units with integral switches that are shared with the entire Panhard range and are also used in the AMX tank and armoured personnel carrier. Therefore, after some careful hunting on the internet they can be sourced.

The 24-volt electrics are powered from two large batteries that sit behind the driver. The vehicle has a 'generator' or dynamo (there is no alternator), so it relies on the batteries to a greater extent. Connecting two large batteries of at least a 45 amp, cold cranking in series will suffice. Choosing a battery by its size is more of an issue than its output, because they have to fit in a very tight mounting box. I found two batteries designed for a large 4 x 4 were just the ticket.

Surprisingly, the cover for the batteries is very difficult to remove. It is harder still if the driver's seat and turret basket are in place, because you have to remove one or the other to get the cover off successfully. Therefore, to avoid having to access the batteries regularly, it may be best to hook up some wires to the batteries that emerge from the side of this cover so they can be linked up to a battery charger/conditioner. If you need a more powerful 'jump-start' for the vehicle, these wires won't suffice, but you can use the jump start socket at the bottom of the fuse box. This socket allows you to charge/discharge the batteries without having to remove them from the vehicle.

By way of a top tip, after using the vehicle make sure you isolate the battery with the switch on the dash, as leaving this open (or indeed the ignition on) will spell doom for the batteries (and probably your coil, too). Therefore the 'turn-off' procedure for the AML must include switching off the ignition system (basically, stopping the engine) and then isolating the battery. This makes a very load 'click' as it isolates so you are audibly and visually reminded everything is disengaged.

The only non-original electrical items I have added to my AMLs have been electronic fuel pumps and cut-off valves. One needs to prime the engine with fuel if not used for prolonged periods and you can use an electronic fuel pump for this. You will also need to shut off the fuel when 'winding down' after use. The fuel cut-off valve will also enable you to stop fuel flow immediately in the event of an emergency. Please remember, fuel being pumped over the top of a hot engine in an enclosed metal 'box' is a recipe for disaster. I would recommend looking into the engine bay before starting or restarting an armoured car to check for fuel leaks or a potential build-up of fuel vapour – one spark could create a very loud bang in a very small space.

To help monitor/control the fuel supply, I have added a fuel pressure regulator and transparent fuel bowl filter. This is vital to ensure the correct fuel flow pressure and to keep an eye on any sediment that may be dragged up from your fuel tank (especially after vigorous off-road driving).

Engine gearbox

Safety note – *the bulkhead between the engine bay and fighting compartment is lined with asbestos and must not be disturbed. I have sealed this asbestos in the past with many thick*

ABOVE Eland petrol overhead valve water-cooled engine.

layers of paint to stabilise it. Fortunately, unlike some armoured vehicles there is no asbestos 'bandage' or cladding on the engine that you need worry about. In a Panhard all asbestos is pressed into boards. Although asbestos particles becoming airborne by simply driving the vehicle is very unlikely, if the panels are disturbed or disintegrate, this could create a problem. I'm sure I don't need to emphasise the fact that asbestos fibre inhalation can result in disease and eventual death.

The same engine is used in both the AML 60 and 90. It's a Panhard-designed and built air-cooled flat-four boxer engine – very similar

BELOW Rear engine bay access of AML, with inspection doors removed and engine in situ.

to a VW Beetle in design – but obviously it has four cylinders. Being developed from the racing version of the Panhard engine it is very high revving, very light in weight and a thoroughbred. As with any thoroughbreds, it cannot be abused and can become temperamental if not cared for correctly.

Being air cooled, the engine relies on good oil circulation to assist this cooling. Therefore oil must be changed regularly (as there is no separate removable oil filter to speak of) and replaced with a high-quality semi-synthetic, reputable, branded oil. I would suggest oil changes at 2,000km or every 12 months, whichever is sooner. The engine has a conventional dipstick so periodic checking is easy.

Failure of any major components in the engine or gearbox will result in the need for complete removal. It makes sense to remove and replace the engine and gearbox together as lining up a clutch inside a cramped hull is extremely difficult.

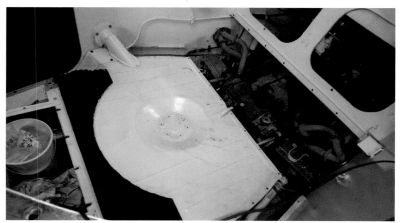

The engine and gearbox may be light, but it is a tricky unit to take out and put back in. The later Eland addressed this issue by placing the engine on a set of rails so the gearbox and engine could be slid out to work on or change. In the Panhard the gearbox and engine are bolted to the hull floor and the whole unit is held against the sides of the hull with a 'nest' of pipes, venting and feeding each of the four cylinders.

To remove the gearbox from its drive shafts in the side of the hull does need two specialist tools, but after stripping a number of these vehicles I found a simple way that does not require them. You can disconnect the final drive station at the rear of the vehicle from the side of the hull – take out the prop-shafts and let these sit loosely on the floor. If you lift the engine, slightly tilted to right or left, you can prize the final drives off with a bar.

To extract the engine from the hull it must be partially dismantled. Exhaust pipes should be uncoupled (some of which are in effect under the engine) and the air filters and carb removed. The entire rear of the vehicle also needs to be dismantled, including a very fiddly air ducting system that houses the large cooling fan. To gain suitable access to the engine bay you need to remove the entire rear armoured plate (that contains the engine bay access hatches). It's also advisable to remove the exhaust baffler above this panel and have the turret rotated at least 90° so you can lift it all out easily. It's a very time-consuming and laborious exercise.

The engine will also need a specialist tool to lift it out at an angle (about 33°). I have used a forklift and lifting straps when this tool was not available, but it is a very fiddly exercise to get the angle just right.

I would advise owners to remove the turret to aid in engine/gearbox removal, the access is then far superior and makes the engine easier to disassemble if you approach it from the crew compartment. Imagine trying to achieve an engine change on exercise or in a combat situation. It must have been an army mechanic's worst nightmare. It certainly kept me awake at night.

The gearbox is a difficult item to fix or source so it's really imperative you are able to secure a decent gearbox with, or already installed in, any vehicle you intend to restore. There are broken units on the market and second-hand units of unknown condition could be as much as 2,000 to 3,000 Euros. I believe new gearboxes are available, but the last price I was quoted in about 2018 was 7,000 Euros.

The gearbox must be treated with respect: grinding of gears or sudden gear changes without adequate clutch use will result in broken or sheared teeth. Therefore, I would suggest a lesson in gearbox use by an experienced driver would be very worthwhile before driving an AML for the first time.

Of course, one can replace the engine (as many nations have) with a post-market diesel or a petrol-powered unit, but this will involve extensive remodelling of the rear engine compartment to accommodate the water cooling equipment.

The carburettor for the engine is a 38 NDIX Solex. This unit is readily available as it was also used on the Panhard road car, the Simca truck series and the Porsche 911. Rebuild kits are available off the shelf at a relatively low price.

Fuel system

The fuel tank sits on the floor of the hull and holds 350 litres. You will need to put in at least 25 litres (from empty) to even register on the dipstick (the AML never had an electronic fuel gauge, you 'dip the tank' from the outside of the vehicle). The French knew these were thirsty vehicles so this is probably why so many have low mileage when released from service.

The fuel tanks do suffer from a build-up of sediment and rusting and are difficult to clean. The tank has literally dozens of baffles, so if your fuel tank is clogged it will need removing, bathing in acid and treating – washing through will not suffice. There is very little that can be done to address an unserviceable fuel tank while it is still in situ – believe me I have tried. To remove the fuel tank the turret needs to be lifted off. Unfortunately there is no other way of removing it from the hull as it is bigger than any hatches, openings or doors.

The main fuel tank feeds a header tank above the engine (above the hot engine!) through a complex pipe and overflow system. The fuel is pumped mechanically to the header tank and is then fed to the carb by gravity,

controlled by a manual tap and an electronic valve. Of all the Panhards I have worked on, these header tanks all seem to have been bypassed by the military and the fuel fed directly from the fuel pump to the carb. This seems a sensible approach but it can lead to over fuelling of the carb, so it is good practice to pass via a pressure regulator and a good-quality fuel filter before delivery to the carb. (I believe the header tanks were to supply the vehicle if the fuel pump failed or the main fuel tank was holed in a combat situation.)

As mentioned before I have now removed the mechanical fuel pump and replaced it with an electronic unit so I can easily prime the engine before use and cut off the fuel flow when I need to stop the engine.

Perhaps if you have a corroded or clogged main fuel tank, you could explore fitting a replacement for the fuel header tank and feed the carb this way. It holds about a dozen litres, so it can support a few short journeys. This would cut out any issues you have with the main fuel tank completely.

Lastly, you will need to use a high-quality fuel, especially if you are not intending to drive the vehicle regularly. The high ethanol content in cheaper fuels can destroy the older rubber seals in the fuel lines and carb. So unless you are consuming the fuel quickly, so it doesn't sit around for long (which, to be honest, it never does in a thirsty Panhard!) you want a good-quality fuel with a high RON that will not degrade or attack these rubber components. I always drain and replace the fuel in the tanks completely when I restore French vehicles as I find their petroleum seems to go stale very quickly, probably because their ethanol and petroleum mix is different than in the UK.

Running gear

In my experience the running gear seems bullet proof, quite literally. If the lubricating oil is clear, it should be okay internally. I always check (and clean off) the front ball joint seals to examine oil loss (high levels of loss manifests itself as wet run marks on the inside of the tyres). The portal axle units/wheel stations need to be filled with Ep90 oil, but there are four dipsticks in the interior/back of the wheel stations to test these levels. White mayonnaise-like deposits or

The propshafts are internal to the hull, so need to be greased well and can make noise when rotating at speed, but this is normal. It would be advisable to check the flail guards are still in place, so any failure of the props will not result in injury to any passengers. They run between the fuel tank and the hull wall.

Brakes on the Panhard are of the drum type, with two brake cylinders per wheel. These can suffer from under- *and* overuse – underused and the braking system will not activate or will apply itself permanently; overuse can heat the drums up and the brakes can start to tighten and eventually lock on. It is well known that the Panhard front brakes can over-cook, therefore use of the foot brake needs to be sparing. Trying not to apply the footbrake is very difficult as it is located under the left foot of the driver. Therefore there is a tendency to dab the brake every time you try to change gear, as your inbuilt driving reflexes believe the brake to be a clutch pedal – and, of course, there is no clutch pedal on an AML. The brake cylinders are standard Lockheed units and can be easily rebuilt.

Constructed from steel and alloy units bolted together, the braking master cylinder is the weak spot in the braking system. It sits on the floor of the Panhard hull, to the very front of the vehicle. If the vehicle fills up with water (as discussed before) and is not drained sufficiently, this unit will become partially submerged and

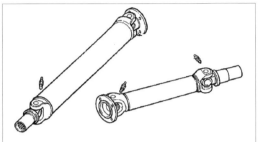

ABOVE AND RIGHT
The driveshaft to rear wheel station runs down a channel next to fuel tank (above). There are two prop-shafts on each side (right).

rust on these dipsticks will indicate if water has entered the wheel stations and they will need to be inspected closely. To top up these units there are filler bolt heads inside the hull and small filler holes in the centre of each wheel hub (accessible from outside the vehicle).

BELOW AND BELOW RIGHT The rear wheel station of the AML utilises drum brakes that are actuated by two cylinders. Inside the hub is oil that lubricates the bearings, which is topped up through a central port.

Internal AML braking pedal and accelerator (left). In this unrefurbished view the brake fluid reservoir has been snapped off (laying horizontally) by a clumsy driver (below). The correct protective box has been added, with the brake pedal on the left, the accelerator on the right.

will start to corrode, drastically reducing its operating life.

The master cylinder activates the front brakes first, then initiates the rear braking – doing all of this from a reducing-diameter bore with two different sized inline pistons. Therefore, if you have a unit that's broken or corroded and wish to rebuild, you must note there are two differing diameters to maintain in the main bore.

The brake master cylinder has also two rather delicate plastic reservoirs to its top. These are usually covered by a robust metal box (I have painted these red in the past so it is clearly visible). This box sits between the driver's feet. Many times I have seen this box going missing or is taken by souvenir hunters. If a larger person enters the vehicle with big booted feet – it is not unknown to snap the fragile reservoirs off the top of the master cylinder rendering the unit unserviceable. Therefore always keep the master cylinder and reservoirs covered as you will inevitably bash this unit as you enter and exit the vehicle!

The Africans recognised this development area and moved the brake mechanism off the floor and placed the reservoirs near the dash board, feeding the master cylinder by pipe.

Wheels and tyres

Wheels and tyres are not readily available. The tyres (Michelin XLs) can be replaced by remanufactured bar treads as used on wartime vehicles (*eg* Dodge WC series) but the overall stance of the vehicle is altered. The tyres have solid nitrogen-filled inner tubes, so any changes of tyres and rims will need specialist support or at least a sympathetic commercial lorry tyre company. Tyres can suffer from 'crazing' to the walls but are quite durable on the whole and shouldn't give you issue.

The wheels with tyres are heavy and quite an effort to lift or change, but being run flats, at least if the driver experiences a puncture he can continue to drive the vehicle with relative ease. Top tip, if you have a door mounted spare tyre, do not try to remove this unaided, as the tyre is at least a two-man lift.

Interior fittings (hull)

There really aren't that many internal fittings to the hull. Once the floor has been refitted and the partition hatches between the engine bay and fighting compartment are accounted for, there is simply a driver's seat, battery cover, dashboard and assorted simple boxes to hold items of kit. Each of these boxes or storage units are easy to remanufacture if missing.

The one item that cannot be remanufactured easily is the steering mechanism. These are removable to allow quick exit from the vehicle. They are removed by simply turning a toothed locking nut in the middle of the steering wheel. Therefore being hand operated and easy to 'undo' they do go missing due to souvenir hunters, or hidden by good friends 'as a laugh' while at military vehicle shows.

These steering units have a multitude of planetary gears within the alloy casing and therefore are extremely hard to reproduce. DO make sure you obtain one of these steering units (and a spare if possible) before considering any restoration.

The gearstick mechanism runs along the entire length of the vehicle and is bolted to the floor. In effect this unit is a long steel bar that pushes back under the fuel tank and is connected by a cranked lever to the front of the gearbox. It is very hard to access. This gear shift being fabricated from mild steel and running inside tight bronze collars, will create problems even with a modicum of corrosion on its surface. It is good practice to regularly oil and grease this gearshift bar as it is vulnerable to moisture.

The gearshift lever has a spring loaded knob that has an electrical contact within its body (in effect the clutch activator). Therefore it is good to check this is in place/works when purchasing a vehicle. Depressing the knob will throw a solenoid at the gearbox and make an audible 'click'. The solenoid has a relay that is attached to the top left-hand side of the clutch bell housing. This relay MUST be in place to operate the gearbox correctly. It has an adjustable knob on the relay to increase its output, but if this is missing you will not be able to change gear effectively.

Interior fittings (turret)

The turret and basket occupies the majority of the space within the AML hull. It is a very simple tubular steel design and easily restored. The only difficulty is with any moving part of the seat mechanism. They can seize as they corrode, being exposed to water entering through the turret hatches. Soaking in penetrating oil, heating vigorously (not necessarily in that order!) then 'assisting' with a large lump hammer can get these units working again.

The seat raising mechanism on the commander's position is a little more difficult to free up if seized as it has quite a few moving parts, but patience and elbow grease will work wonders.

As the operators of AMLs used their seats as foot steps to get in and out the turret, these wooden-based seat squabs do break and may well need replacing. They are easily reproduced as they are nothing more than a simple wooden disk with padding and a cover. Any classic car interior specialist would be able to remanufacture replacement items easily.

Sights and vision blocks

The Panhard uses two types of vision blocks. They are known in France as 'episcopes' or 'lunettes' by their nomenclatures of 'APX L794B' and 'APX L794D'. One is shorter (B), the other is longer (D) and the latter has small cross hairs

engraved on the glass. These are readily found on internet auction sites as they were used in a wide range of armoured vehicle. Indeed they were designed, based on those used in Second World War German tanks, and sometimes are sold as such. There is no issue finding these episcopes, and they are relatively cheap singularly. Unfortunately the cost does start to mount, as you can need between 11 and 14 of them depending on turret. Of course these are not key to restoring or driving the vehicle, but I feel at least the three of the driver's position helps 'finish off' the driver's hatch nicely.

The AML 60 has a mortar sighting periscope, and the AML 90 has a main gun telescope. Both of these items are extremely hard to locate. The nomenclatures are primarily APX M112 and APX M262 respectively, but there are many others depending on the turret armament fitted or type of sight needed.

These were not generally released to the public by the French military, as they constituted part of the armament. Some have ended up in private collections or museums, but their rarity means they command a good price. The last M112 sights I saw available for sale cost in excess of 500 Euros.

Radios/communications

Both vehicles utilise standardised radio equipment that originated from the US forces. Most US radio kit was basically copied by the French after the Second World War. You will find at least two differing radio systems in the Panhard. In the earlier vehicles you will find the GRC 9 (Angry 9 of Second World War fame) and the later RT-68 GRC. Both of these units are readily available, although searching for working units with French markings is a tad harder. The French had the penchant, in the past, for enthusiastically smashing their radio set internals before releasing the cases on to the open market. This can make for an unpleasant surprise when you decide to open up your newly purchased shiny radio case to see why it is not working properly. Fortunately there are many collectors and dealers of such radios and finding at least an American version will not be hard.

If you wish to ensure your turret ancillaries are working (*eg* the fume extractor fan, internal lights, radio and intercom system), you will need to ensure you have the rotational power unit that sits in the middle of the fighting compartment floor. It looks rather like an old portable television set, but it effectively transmits

electricity and intercom signals from the vehicle chassis to the rotating turret.

These are very complex pieces of kit, so it's best to ensure your vehicle has one.

The AML does not have any electric turret rotation or gun laying apparatus, everything is manual, so unlike track laying tanks of the same period, there is little hydraulic or electrical turret movement issues to worry about.

Weapon systems

I have found AML 60s nearly always have their main armaments removed when offered for sale. The weapon systems are easy to remove (the 60mm mortar and the two co-axial machine guns), therefore replacing these items with either deactivated units or replicas is straightforward. The only consideration is the cost. If you have a turret that houses the two French AA-52s they can costs 2,000 Euros each. I have found very suitable reproduction machine guns made from laser-cut steel easy to fit. These only cost a few hundred pounds and certainly look the part.

AML 90s nearly always have their main armament still in situ. These guns will need either to be licensed if still live (with a firearms certificate) or deactivated to the appropriate level with accompanying UK (and for the foreseeable future, European) paperwork.

ABOVE AND BELOW The turret electrical 'box' rotates on the hull floor to continue feeding the turret, no matter what direction the armament is facing. An Eland undergoes refurbishment at the Sandock-Austral facility at Boksburg near Johannesburg – restoration on an industrial scale..

The deactivation of the main 90mm weapon is not greatly intrusive, but will render the breech probably inoperative, and of course the barrel will be blocked. Bear in mind a blocked barrel will mean it could fill with rainwater at the back of the 'plug' – hence it is good procedure to follow the practice of the French Army and use a canvas cover over the recoil compensator to keep out the weather.

These barrels can be easily enhanced to support simulated gunfire. This can be delivered by using pyrotechnics inside the barrel or by 'gassing' the main armament. Gassing is a process by which propane and oxygen mix is injected into the barrel and ignited – this gives a very satisfactory 'bang' and muzzle flash. Don't try to accomplish this without the correct kit and installation advice given by professionals. To be in a confined turret filled with ignited propane is not good for you – or anything else flammable.

The AML 60 carried a large number of mortar rounds (over 40 in various boxes and racks around the turret basket wall) and thousands of machine-gun rounds in ammunition boxes. The AML 90 could carry up to 25 rounds in its turret racking, vertically around its occupants and behind the commander in tubes. To replicate a fully-armed AML can start to get pricey as a single deactivated round for the 90mm gun can be as much as £300, and a simple 60mm deactivated mortar round can be about £40.

I have personally commissioned wooden replicas of each type of round based on an original inert example. Once in their positions and painted accordingly these are surprisingly effective.

The vehicles also have designated 'clips' that hold the side arms belonging to the crew. These initially took the form of MAT-49 sub-machine pistols. In the door is a receiving bracket as well as two built into the back of the turret baskets. These are also available deactivated, but can be a challenge to source.

Lastly there were several 'cubby holes' in the hull and turret that held grenades. These were for use by the AML occupants for self-defence purposes.

Tools and personal equipment

One of the most pleasing elements of any refurbishment I have found is sourcing and attaching the pioneer tools, specialist tools and personal equipment.

The axe, shovel and mattock that adorn the front glacis plate, are of a type that were general issue to the French forces. Connoisseurs look for items with the correct markings, for example stampings that proclaim 'Armée Francais', but being standard shape and sizes, alternatives can still be found in hardware shops on your local high street.

The sand channels that are attached at the front of the vehicle are slightly harder to locate. These were direct copies of the British Army postwar sand channel, and can be found being sported on the front of many restored British Army Ferrets. The Panhard holds these items (there are two bolted together) channel side inwards, and you find the Eland hold these channel side outwards. This can be a quick way of recognising these two similar vehicles apart from a distance. These channels, although once plentiful, are now harder to locate and can become expensive. To that end some enterprising individuals have started reproducing copies that are very similar to the originals.

The AML also carried on the hull a steel rope draped from bow to stern. These can be easily remanufactured. The one Panhard peculiarity are the attachment shackles that hold the wire rope in position and were also used for tethering or lifting the vehicle. The Panhard shackle is quite specific and fits snugly into a number of receiving brackets dotted around the hull (three at the bow, two amidships, four to the stern and two atop the front shock absorbers). These are slim C-shaped shackles with a straight locking pin at the bottom. They were also used on the Panhard EBR so these are interchangeable. Again with searches on the internet they can be found.

In the engine bay under the left access hatch we have a portable compressor that affixes to the rear of the vehicle to provide a system to reinflate the tyres. Under the right-hand rear access hatch for the engine bay is a box containing the tyre inflation 'gun' and associated hose. These two items, if missing, can be tricky to locate, but sometimes they appear on internet auction websites.

As you'd expect there are a number of hand tools that appear in the rear lockers in a fully-equipped AML. These are very similar to those used in most French Army military vehicles of the period. The most surprising looking tool is one that closely resembles a 1950s lavatory brush. It took me a while to work out its use – it turns out it's used for cleaning the backs of the front wheels after off-road use. I think I would insult your intelligence if I started to tell you what the sponge was used for.

The engine does use a number of very specialist tools, as does the fuel cap. The fuel cap is removed by a cruciform tool that has varying hexagonal drive profiles on the end of each arm. The fuel cap once removed has a secondary cap behind it made from bronze – this will need the cruciform tool to remove it as well. A good tip is not to lose this tool. It is also needed to remove the engine sump plug, the hull drain plugs and can lock the doors and hatches from the outside to stop unauthorised entry. In effect it's your 'car key'.

The spark plugs are awkward to remove (the original shielded versions) and you will need a very precise cranked spanner for this. It helps to locate an original spanner and have a copy made at least. Without this tool at that special cranked angle it is near impossible to remove the shielded spark plugs from the engine successfully.

Held in the rear wing lockers, tied up in a canvas roll, are the usual myriad of spanners, hammers, pliers and screwdrivers – again, all very similar to those used for French military soft-skin vehicles of the period. This can become a very detailed field of collecting. The larger of the rear wing lockers houses the heavy 'jump cable' to charge or discharge the vehicle's batteries. Inside the hull we have spaces for first-aid tins and the gas masks – as well as brackets to hold the spare vision blocks.

On AML 60s and many AML 90s you can also find a 20-litre Jerrycan in a carrying basket on the right-hand hull door. The Jerrycan is the direct copy of the German original design, but they alter just slightly by having their breather pipes to the exterior of what is the wide-necked filler spout. These are readily available. Look out for dated ones with the various different manufacturers' markings – or indeed ones with 'VIN' stamped into them. Yes that's right – a fuel can specifically designed to carry wine! These are French vehicles after all.

On the exterior of the right-hand door and inside the hull next to the driver, you will find the brackets to hold the French Army pressurised decontaminator. Decontaminators were considered 'weapons' by the French authorities and were mostly destroyed as part of their deactivation. A small number have reached the collectors' market, but because of their attachment on the later Hotchkiss M201 Jeep they are in great demand. They look very similar to bulbous fire extinguishers in green, but have a distinctive neck and brass valve at the mouth.

Both vehicles utilised the 'antenne embase AB-15/GR'. These are brown porcelain aerial bases, with a flexible shaft to hold the three- or four-piece whip antennae. There are a number of different variants available, but the same general design was adopted by NATO, so if you can't locate a French one there are German or American versions available you could use.

Particular to both vehicles are the barrel cleaning kits for the 90mm gun and 60mm low-pressure mortar. Both are stored in canvas bags externally on the backs of the turrets. The canvas covers are easily obtainable, but the actual cleaning kits are harder to locate.

To conclude this final section, on both wings of the AMLs you'll find a fire extinguisher and the folding aluminium and glass portable driver's windscreen (with wiper). The extinguishers can be sourced easily as they had lots of applications in the French Army, but the removable windshield is slightly more elusive. It is very similar (if not identical) to the Heath Robinson contraption used on the Panhard EBR. It consists of two fragile aluminium wings with a central glass windscreen that sports a canvas hood and electrically operated windscreen motor.

To use the windscreen unit is rather like putting one's head in a medium-size fish tank. When the erratic windscreen motor sweeps the arm slowly across your line of vision, and the hood has leaked rainwater down your neck (as it has no sealing strip to the hull) you have a tendency to give up on its use. It's no wonder these were rarely utilised. They also break extremely easily as they are constructed from very thin metal and glass. Lastly, they are downright ugly, ruining the well-considered lines of an AML, which I find are, in the main, quite pleasing on the eye.

ABOVE AND RIGHT AML 90 before and after restoration project.

BELOW Baz England-Davis speeds across country at the controls of his immaculate AML 90

Chapter Six

The AML in foreign service

There is no question that the Panhard AML series has been a considerable success on the international arms market, as has the Eland armoured car. Almost 50 nations have adopted the armoured cars and their numerous variants and, after more than 50 years since its inception, many remain in service to this day – the hallmark of a truly exceptional AFV.

OPPOSITE A Panhard AML 90 takes part in a parade to mark the 194th anniversary of El Salvador's independence on 15 September 2015. *(Getty Images)*

121

NATO service

In the NATO alliance the main colonial powers (Britain and France) had both given up most of their colonial aspirations by the early 1960s. Use of armoured cars for reconnaissance work was abandoned in British doctrine in the late 1960s and the CVRT tracked reconnaissance vehicle family was adopted by the Belgians and a number of other countries. West Germany had its own Spähpanzer Luchs under development and the Netherlands employed vehicles of the M113 family and the AMX 13 Mle 58. Only Spain and Portugal purchased the AML, with the intention of employing them in their colonies and with the idea of modernising their NATO reconnaissance units as a secondary aim.

BELOW Humber Mk IV armoured car as employed in all of Portugal's overseas colonies.

AML Portugal

In 1961 the Portuguese Army's cavalry corps included a substantial part of its strength in colonial garrisons, many of which were equipped with armoured cars supplied from wartime stocks by Britain and Canada. The unique exception was the relatively small number of EBRs and ETTs from the order placed in the late 1950s. In Guinea-Bissau a single reconnaissance squadron equipped with 8 GMC Foxes and 5 GMC C15 APCs formed part of the garrison. In Angola a cavalry group incorporating 3 cavalry squadrons (each with 8 Foxes and 15 C15s) was deployed. Some 8 Humber Armoured Cars were based in Macau, with a smaller detachment in Timor. In Mozambique a group of 3 cavalry

RIGHT A heavily modified Daimler Dingo scout car named 'LUISA' is indicative of the ageing AFVs employed by the Portuguese in Angola during the Guerra Ultramar in the 1970s.

reconnaissance squadrons with a total of 21 EBRs and 16 ETTs was operational. Last of all, a detachment comprising 4 cavalry squadrons was operational in Goa, equipped with some 37 Humbers and 16 C15s.

With the exception of the 21 totally unsuitable Panhard EBR FL10s in Mozambique (vehicles designed to protect armoured reconnaissance units from enemy tanks, which the guerilla enemy did not have in Mozambique!), the equipment of the Portuguese cavalry squadrons in Mozambique and Angola was already thoroughly obsolete in the early 1960s. Worn-out Second World War-era armoured cars and M5A1 light tanks were returned regularly to Portugal in increasingly poor condition for repairs and when these proved impossible (due to spares shortages) it drove the army to acquire the AML 60 and the M3 VTT (known in Portugal as the VTBL) from France in the mid-1960s. Portugal encountered many difficulties obtaining modern light AFVs for their African colonial wars, its army operating constantly on a very limited defence budget. Ultimately Portugal produced a small number of Chaimite APCs based closely on a Cadillac Gage design and these were used heavily in Angola and Mozambique, but the AML 60 proved a useful weapon in Africa as many others had discovered.

The three Portuguese Independent Cavalry Reconnaissance Squadrons operational in

CENTRE Undoubtedly Portugal's colonial wars in Africa may be deemed to have been tilting at windmills, but this Portuguese AML 60 strikes a suitable pose for a Panhard publicity brochure soon after the AML was procured by the Portuguese Army.

RIGHT An AML 60 of the 1st Cavalry Regiment of Angola displays the characteristic camouflage scheme of green and brown splotches over the base colour used in the Angolan campaign.

RIGHT An EBR 75 FL10 of the Movimento das Forças Armadas is surrounded by Lisbon citizens during the Carnation Revolution of 25 April 1974. There was a confrontation between an EBR and a regime M47 Patton at the Terreiro do Paço but no shots were fired by either AFV.

Mozambique included the Escuadron de Reconocmiento de Caballeria n. 1. 'Lourenco Marques', the Escuadron de Reconocimiento de Caballeria n. 2. 'Nampula' and the Escuadron de Reconocimietno de Caballeria n. 3. 'Vila Perry'. Each included a Command and Staff Platoon of 48 men with 1 armoured car, 2 armoured personnel carriers, 10 Jeeps, 6 trucks and 3 x 81mm mortars. The fighting power of each was provided by three Reconnaissance Sections of 41 men, each equipped with 2 armoured cars, 1 armoured personnel carrier, 7 Jeeps, and three 60mm mortars. In total, each Portuguese Cavalry Reconnaissance Squadron included 7 armoured cars, 5 armoured personnel carriers, 31 Jeeps, 6 trucks, 9 x 60mm mortars, 3 x 60mm mortars, 5 officers and 176 non-commissioned soldiers. Daimler Dingo, Humber Mk IV armoured cars, EBR 75 FL10, Ferret, and eventually the AML 60 all served in these Escuadron de Reconocmiento de Caballeria. There is some evidence that a number of South African-built Elands armed with 90mm guns were provided to the Portuguese late in the conflict, perhaps as the metropolitan army realised its own NATO commitments would be put at risk if all the AMLs were sent to Africa, for as in Spain the Panhards were an important component of the reconnaissance cavalry force required for national security.

AML Spain

Between 1965 and 1967 Spain purchased 140 AMLs of the H60 and H90 types from Panhard. The two Legion units (GLSh I and GLSh II) serving in the Sahara were the first to be equipped with the AML, and they proved an excellent patrol vehicle. These Legion units each received twelve H60s and six H90s, and the Legion's AMLs were nicknamed *Panarinas*. As other Spanish cavalry units received their cars, they were referred to as *Ranas*, a further abbreviation. Spain was a latecomer to NATO and had suffered from the refusal of several member nations to sell Franco's government any kind of weaponry. France eagerly courted Spanish arms sales throughout the 1960s and 1970s however, and sold Spain a wide range of weapons including the AMX 30B (with a

subsequent production licence) and the AML series. The Spanish Army's Menendez Tolosa army reform modernised many aspects of the military, creating nine Groups of Light Cavalry. These Gruppo de Cabalaria Ligere (GLC I, II, III, IV, V, VI, VII, VIII, IX) were reconnaissance units equivalent in size to armoured squadrons, which were to be equipped with armoured cars. There was one GLC for each of the nine Defence Operational Planning Infantry Brigades (known by the Spanish abbreviation BRIDOT). A further Light Cavalry Group, GLC X, was garrisoned in the Majorcan town of Inca. Two reconnaissance groups of the Saharan Light Corps, Spanish Foreign Legion (GLSh I and II) equipped with the AML were also stationed in the Province of Spanish Western Sahara. The AML also equipped the training establishment then called the RINS 'Calatrava' Pucelano No 2 Training Regiment, located in Pinar, which operated an Escadrón Mixto of two platoons of AMLs, each with a pair of AML H60s and a pair of AML H90s. These cavalry regiments and the Calatrava No 2 instruction regiment organised a series of standardised training procedures to familiarise their crews. The AML also served in the two cavalry regiments that were based in North Africa, the 3rd Montesa Regiment and the 10th Alcantara Regiment, as well as in the Spanish Marine Corps (probably in squadron-sized detachments of 8 to 12 cars). The AML served until the mid-1980s when the BRIDOT system was superseded. When the Spanish Army's AML HL90s were retired their turrets were kept in service, transferred to the hulls of Spanish-built VEC-625 armoured vehicles.

ABOVE An AML 60 leads a column of AFVs including two Panhard EBRs with turrets traversed and two Bravia Chaimite APCs: a Portuguese copy of the Cadillac-Gage V-100 Commando. In the second Chaimite named BULA is the dictator Marcello Caetano who was detained at the main Lisbon military police station on the Largo do Carmo and then escorted out of the city.

RIGHT An AML 90 equipped with SIMFICS of 1st Cavalry Squadron takes part in a military parade. Based at Fermoy, the squadron comprised four AML 90s, six A ML 60s and three M3 APCs. *(Richard Maloney)*

AML Ireland

The Republic of Ireland adopted the AML after participating in United Nations (UN) peacekeeping missions in the Congo with the superannuated Thomson-Ford Mk 6 armoured cars dating from the 1930s. The Irish Army had not yet finished in the Congo when it was tasked with peacekeeping in Cyprus in 1964. With the pressing need of the army finally addressed, 16 AML 60-7s were procured by Ireland that year, two of which were deployed immediately to the UN mission in Cyprus followed by another six shipped directly from France. As tensions in Northern Ireland mounted in 1969–70 with consequent concerns about security on the Republic's border, another 16 AML 60-7s, 20 AML 90s and 60 VTT Panhard M3 APCs were purchased with deliveries between 1972 and 1975.

The M3 APCs were fitted with the Creusot-Loire TL.2.1.80 turret armed with twin FN MAG 7.62mm machine-guns. The procurement of the AML fleet represented one of the most

BELOW With green shamrocks adorning the sides of the turret, an AML 90 of IRISHBATT of UNIFIL supervises the separation of Lebanese and IDF units in the summer of 1978.

significant arms purchases made by the Irish Army since its formation. From 1989, 16 AML 60-7 CS armoured cars' twin 7.62mm machine-guns were replaced with a single M2 Browning .5-inch machine-gun each. After various trials, most of Ireland's AMLs received new Peugeot engines in the late 1990s.

Irish AMLs and M3s served for many years with the UN across the world from Lebanon (UNIFIL) to Liberia (UNIMIL). The deployment of the 43rd Irish Battalion (IRISHBATT) in June 1978 to Lebanon was an arduous undertaking designed to create a neutral buffer zone between the Israel Defense Forces (IDF) and their acolytes the South Lebanon Army (SLA) as well as multifarious insurgent groups such as the PLO. On 6 April clashes began between the IRISHBATT and the SLA in the village of At Tiri in southern Lebanon.

After days of sporadic shelling, SLA militiamen under the odious Major Saad Haddad attacked an Irish UNIFIL checkpoint at Point 615-A in the village of At Tiri on 10 April 1980. During the three-day incident, one Fijian UN peacekeeper was mortally wounded, four others taken prisoner and the checkpoint overrun. The SLA then deployed four M9 halftracks equipped with Browning heavy machine-guns, which they used to harass UNIFIL convoys. Two days later, Irish

AML-90s counter-attacked and retook the village. One halftrack was immobilised and a second destroyed after receiving a direct hit from a 90mm shell. A third was abandoned when its Browning was disabled by warning fire from an AML's co-axial machine gun. The armoured cars also held a tense stand-off with SLA M50 Super Sherman tanks on the outskirts of At Tiri. Although the latter ultimately declined to intervene in the fighting, an AML 90 was rammed causing significant damage. The confrontation continued for

ABOVE Taken from a Super 8 film frame, this IRISHBATT AML 90 was rammed by an SLA M50 Sherman during the incident in At Tiri in April 1980, causing considerable damage.

LEFT In 1992, Manroy Engineering of the UK completed a contract to replace the 60mm mortars in Irish Army AMLs with the Manroy 0.5in (12.7mm) M2 HB QCB (Quick Change Barrel) machine-gun. This entailed removing the mortar and mounting and replacing them with a new mantlet and cradle for the machine-gun. Modifications were also carried out to the sights and ammunition feed systems as well as the ammunition and storage systems. (Anthony Ryan)

RIGHT The Irish Defence Force (IDF) ordered 60 M3 VTT or APC in 1971 and the first 17 were delivered in the following year. The Panhard M3 APC was fitted with a Creusot-Loire TL.21.80 turret armed with twin FN MAG 7.62mm machine-guns. Fourteen of these vehicles served with the IRISHBATT in Lebanon as part of UNIFIL.

72 hours during which time two Irish AML crewmen, Cpl Michael Jones and Pte Michael Daly, were awarded their country's highest bravery award, the Military Medal for Gallantry, for saving wounded comrades under heavy fire. With the arrival of Dutch UNIFIL reinforcements armed with BGM-71 TOW missiles, the SLA forces withdrew.

In 1996, the Panhard M3 was withdrawn from service with the Irish Army and the AML armoured cars in 2013, with any remaining vehicles sold to SOFEMA in 2015.

AML and Eland, Morocco

An AML 90 of the Royal Moroccan Armed Forces modernised with a Peugeot XD3T diesel engine is shown in the distinctive desert camouflage scheme adopted during the protracted war against the Polisario Front in the Western Sahara. Prior to the outbreak of the Western Sahara War in 1975, the Royal Moroccan Armed Forces (FAR) received relatively little modern armament, particularly from non-Francophone states. Meanwhile,

RIGHT The final version of the AML in Irish service was the combination of an AML hull and a South African Denel LIW 20mm gun turret. The G12 20mm cannon has 300 ready rounds with passive night sights and rangefinder housings mounted each side of the gun mantlet.

the Polisario Front, intent on waging an armed struggle for Sahrawi independence, had stockpiled weapons from Algeria and seized additional equipment during raids on Moroccan forces. The hardware attrition rate spiralled upwards after the Madrid Accords and it quickly became apparent that new suppliers were needed to fill the bulk of FAR's needs. A gradual arms build-up in the Sahara began in 1976, and the Moroccans set out in search of arms with generous military grants from Saudi Arabia and other sympathetic

Arab monarchies. FAR procurement officials initially specified a requirement for 200 AMLs in 1976. Panhard and the French government obligingly supplied the FAR with a number of AMLs, including some from surplus French military stocks. However, Panhard was also scaling its production line to refocus on the AML's successor, the six-wheeled ERC. The Moroccans were referred to South Africa, which agreed to fulfil the remaining balance of the order. The first Eland Mk 6s were clandestinely imported between late 1976 and early 1978

ABOVE An AML 90 of the Royal Moroccan Armed Forces modernised with a Peugeot XD3T diesel engine is shown in the distinctive desert camouflage scheme adopted during the protracted war against the Polisario Front in the Western Sahara.

LEFT Polisario Panhard AFVs captured from the Moroccan Army lie abandoned after the conflict with a variety of versions including AML 90, Eland Mk 6 and Eland 20.

under a veil of absolute secrecy, as Morocco was a member of the Organization of African Unity, which had prohibited trade with South Africa among its constituent states. As per the FAR's request, Sandock Austral agreed to censor all domestic markings from the Elands prior to their export. The Elands were simply referred to as Reconnaissance Vehicle Mk 6 in the training materials supplied with them. They were accompanied by eight South African instructors for training the FAR crews, although like the Elands their presence in the country was a closely guarded secret. All FAR personnel not involved directly in the training programme were forbidden to approach them. Polisario Panhard AFVs captured from the Moroccan army lie abandoned after the conflict with a variety of versions including AML 90, Eland Mk 6 and Eland 20. In September 1979, the FAR adopted a new strategy under General Ahmed Dlimi of consolidating the occupation forces spread out across Western Sahara into mobile tactical groups for massed search and destroy operations against Polisario forces near Dakhla, Zag and Tarfaya. The FAR Elands were first deployed during Operation 'Imam', one such offensive to break the Polisario encirclement of Zag. Their crews proceeded through a narrow valley against the counsel of their South African instructors, who correctly suspected a Polisario ambush. A large insurgent force was able to trap and cut off the column of armoured cars in the valley, inflicting catastrophic losses. Over 30 Elands were captured during the failed offensive and a smaller number destroyed. The South Africans had not been as thorough with censoring their domestic markings as they believed, and upon close inspection the curious insurgents found Afrikaans inscriptions on the Elands' intact filler caps. The captured Elands were pressed into service by the Polisario forces for a number of years, although their latter years of service were limited mostly to Polisario military parades in El Aaiún.

AML and Eland, Mali

As part of the African International Support Mission to Mali (AFISMA), the formidable fighters of the Chadian Army and their Eland Mk 6 armoured cars prepared for action in the Kidal area against Islamist militants in northern Mali in support of Operation 'Serval'. The latter was a UN-sponsored military offensive undertaken by French armed forces between January 2013 and July 2014 to underpin the Malian government. With support from 16 other UN nations, the French deployed a range of AFVs including AMX 10 RC and Panhard ERC Sagaie armoured cars as well as VAB and VBCI APCs. In conjunction with French forces, these Eland armoured cars spearheaded the attack on 30 January 2013 against Kidal, the last town in Mali to be held by AQIM (Al-Qaeda Islamic Maghreb). Despite extensive training from South African advisers, the Chads employed their Eland armoured cars in only one way – in a headlong cavalry charge, often in conjunction with 'technicals' armed with Dushkas or MILAN ATGW as well as heavy plant equipment in a fearful combination. The Serval (Leptailurus Serval) is a wild cat native to Africa and was also the name given to a late model AML armoured car.

AML Zaire

Formerly the Belgian Congo and latterly the Democratic Republic of Congo, Zaire procured 95 AML armoured cars in the early 1970s for the Forces Armées Zaïroise or FAZ. However, FAZ troops were poorly trained and rarely paid so their performance in battle was mediocre particularly during the Shaba campaign of March and May 1977. An invasion of the mineral rich Katanga province by the Front for the National Liberation of the Congo (FNLC), supported by the Angolan MPLA, was only contained by a force of Moroccan troops flown in by the French Air Force. Here, a FAZ AML 90 advances along a road during Shaba I. In the following year, another invasion known as Shaba II by the FNLC was readily thwarted by the formidable combination of the 2ème Régiment Étranger de Parachutistes and the Belgian 1er Para-Commando Régiment. In the Battle of Kolwezi, the insurgents attacked with three captured AML armoured cars at 15.00hrs on 19 May 1978. The commanders were killed by FR F1 sniper fire and one vehicle destroyed by LRAC F1 rocket launchers, both brand new weapons to the légionnaires at that time.

ABOVE As part of the African International Support Mission to Mali (AFISMA), the formidable fighters of the Chadian army and their Eland Mark 6 armoured cars prepare for action in the Kidal area against Islamist militants in northern Mali in support of Operation Serval.
(Getty Images)

LEFT A camouflaged FAZ AML 60 advances along a road during Shaba 1 in 1977.

RIGHT The AML 90s of the Argentine Army were later modified with a laser rangefinder for the fire-control system, as evident above the barrel of the 90mm gun.

Argentina

Sixty AML H90 units were acquired by Argentina from France between 1977 and 1978, to re-equip the cavalry reconnaissance squadrons located across the country. During the Beagle Channel dispute with Chile in late November 1978, the cavalry reconnaissance squadrons were ordered to mobilise but saw no combat. At the outbreak of the conflict in the South Atlantic in April 1982, the squadrons mobilised for imminent deployment on the understanding that their AMLs were far more suitable to operate in the Falklands than the TAM (Tanque Argentino Mediano), AMX 13 Mle 58 or other tank type employed by the army. This was quickly proven to be a miscalculation, for much of the ground proved impassable to any wheeled vehicle.

On the cool morning of 2 April 1982, officers and men of the 181st Reconnaissance Detachment of Armoured Cavalry Regiment 3 'General Angel Pacheco' (today's Cavalry Reconnaissance Regiment 3) formed up in the Plaza de Armas in the barracks at Esquel, in Chubut province, Argentina. Their commander, Cavalry Lt Col Jorge Raúl Spinetta, made a surprising announcement to his men: Argentina had 'reconquered' the Malvinas, the long-coveted Falkland Islands. The detachment, and eight of its AML 90s, would be employed to reinforce the islands' newly emplaced Argentinian garrison.

LEFT Sub-Lt Fernando Chércoles, commander of Cobra Section, and Cabo (L/Cpl) Castillo service the AA-52 7.62mm machine-gun atop their AML 90 at Moody Brook in the typical barren terrain of the Falkland Islands during May 1982. On 1 May, this weapon fired the detachment's first shots in anger at an attacking Harrier aircraft flying at low altitude. In the driver's compartment is Soldado (Private) Cape Vilte who saved the life of Lt Gustavo Adolfo Tamanos when the latter was seriously wounded in a British artillery and aerial bombardment during the battle for Wireless Ridge on 12 June 1982. *(Jose Luis Calvo)*

The detachment was composed of two AML 90 sections, one of which headed up each reconnaissance squadron. Squadron A at the time had five AML 90s on strength, while Squadron B had recently received orders to transfer one AML 90 to another unit, and had only four cars on strength. The detachment commander ordered the two sections combined for the operation under the command of 2/Lt Gustavo Adolfo Tamanos. An intensive period of training commenced immediately in order to prepare the detachment's conscripts for war.

A convoy including the nine armoured cars was driven to Comodoro Rivadavia airport on 5 April, 600km away. One AML 90 broke down en route and was recovered to Esquel. The rest of the detachment were issued supplies for use in theatre and their cars and crews were prepared for loading aboard C-130 Hercules aircraft in pairs, to be flown in relays to the newly renamed Malvinas.

The AML crews had no experience in airlift operations, but backed the AML 90s into the C-130's gaping hold. Air force loadmasters lashed the fully stowed vehicles to the floor of the aircraft. Together the two AMLs weighed about 12 tonnes in combat order, and were small enough that a third might have fitted in had the length of the landing strip not limited the aircraft's all-up weight. The three subsequent days were marked by flights carrying six more AMLs in an operation that had never even been attempted previously

ABOVE Festooned with vegetation to mask its outlines, the AML 90 of the commander of Eagle Section, Lt Gustavo Adolfo Tamanos, drives along Ross Road West on 12 June 1982 towards the frontlines on the first day the Panhards went into action. Just hours later this vehicle was badly damaged by British artillery fire near Wireless Ridge. The crew comprising 2-Lt Tamanos, Cabo Alegre and Soldado Inglesias were all wounded. The total casualties of Armoured Cavalry Exploration Detachment 181 were just five injured during the war.

by the Argentinian Air Force. The AMLs were accompanied by 2 officers, 12 NCOs and 13 soldiers of the 181st Reconnaissance Detachment, who were quickly joined by other reconnaissance troops.

Two AML 90s from the 9th Armoured Cavalry Reconnaissance Squadron from Rio Mayo in the same province were flown out to the Malvinas over the next days. Two more AMLs from the 10th Armoured Cavalry Reconnaissance Squadron from La Tablada, Buenos Aires, followed, raising the total number of AMLs sent to the Malvinas to twelve. They were, along with VAO (LVTP7 Amphibious Vehicles Caterpillar), the only armoured vehicles sent by the Argentinian High Command to the archipelago during the conflict. A request made to send some SK-105 Kürassiers failed to develop further because of the British naval blockade.

Once on the islands the AML 90s were expected to provide mobile fire support to infantry forces already in place around Port Stanley. The strategic mobility of the lightweight AML was well

demonstrated, and the British had no idea that the Argentinians were capable of airlifting any AFVs on to the islands. The British naval blockade prevented any other Argentinian ambitions of reinforcing the troops on the islands with tracked AFVs (they could have sent more powerfully armed SK105s, AMX 13s or TAM medium tanks had any sea lift opportunity presented itself). Wheeled vehicles faced serious disadvantages on the muskeg-covered Falklands and the AMLs bogged as easily as any army lorry.

The Panhard squadron was divided into two groups of six AMLs. 'Eagle' detachment, commanded by Lt Gustavo Adolfo Tamanos and 'Cobra' detachment, commanded by 2/Lt Fernando Pedro Chércoles were active through the remainder of the conflict. The squadron was commanded by Maj Carullo. Because of the soft ground, their movements were restricted to a few gravel roads and paved areas near the capital, which allowed just a few kilometres of road movements. In that sense, the CVRT light tanks Scorpion FV101 and FV107 Scimitar, used by the British, were more suitable vehicles. The tasks assigned in the early days of the war and throughout the month of May were primarily road-bound reconnaissance.

On more than one occasion the AMLs ended up buried in the peat up to their axles and it

was necessary to use a Chinook helicopter to lift the trapped Panhards out. Moreover, moisture and cold, typical of the islands, caused damage to the electrical systems and forced crews to almost always preheat vehicle batteries. Another drawback presented to the Panhard crew was their lack of night vision sights and goggles, which rendered them useless during actions in hours of darkness.

After the British landed, the AML squadron served as a mobile reserve stationed in the area of the racecourse, to counter the enemy advance on Wireless Ridge and Moody Brook on 12, 13 and 14 June 1982. While the AML 90s never exchanged fire with the Blues and Royals' CVRTs, some were detached and were used in combat against the 3rd Battalion, the Parachute Regiment on 12 and 13 June 1982 at Sapper Hill (inflicting some of the 6 dead and 70 wounded suffered by the British in this engagement). Despite wounds many of the crewmen from the 3rd, 9th and 10th Cavalry Reconnaissance Regiments fought on in full knowledge that their positions were by now untenable.

Artillery and naval gunfire damaged several of the AMLs and drove the Argentinians from their positions and to retreat into Port Stanley. They covered the withdrawal of Argentinian troops in the area once the British advanced on Wireless

LEFT After the 1982 war, the remaining AMLs were nicknamed 'Perla Austral' or 'Pearl of the South' for the rest of their careers in the Argentinian Army as recognition of their participation in La Guerra Malvinas. Note the 'Sun of May' national insignia on the turret side of this AML 90, named 'LEOPARDO', that served with the Escuadron Salta.

Ridge, attracting British artillery fire and air strikes by Harrier aircraft and British helicopters. Two AMLs were damaged by shrapnel, the crew of one being badly injured when shrapnel ruptured a fuel tank. Both AMLs were immobilised, their tyres destroyed by shrapnel, even though their guns could continue operating.

With the capitulation on 14 June the Panhards were rendered partially unusable. The breech blocks of their 90mm guns were removed as well as some other components. Thus disarmed, the AML 90s were driven in column to the side street next to Port Stanley's Globe Hotel and surrendered to the British. One of the Panhards, EA33524 named 'Teniente Coronel Olascoaga', was shipped and transported to England to be put on display at the Tank Museum, Bovington. The remaining 48 AMLs carried the nickname 'Perla Austral' for the rest of their careers in Argentinian service.

In January 1989, the Panhard AML H90s of the 10th Armoured Cavalry Reconnaissance Regiment from La Tablada were employed to recover the regiment's base after its takeover by subversive elements of the resurgent People's Revolutionary Army. During the actions, the vehicles fired several times on the guerilla positions, including illegal white phosphorous rounds, until their total annihilation.

BELOW On 23 January 1989, the Panhard AML H90s of the Escuadron de Exploracion Caballeria Blindada 10 (10th Armoured Cavalry Reconnaissance Squadron) were employed to recover La Tablada base of the 3rd Mechanised Infantry Regiment after its capture by fighters of the Movimiento Todos por la Patria or MTP (All for the Motherland Movement). The MTP assault was intended to pre-empt an alleged military coup against the national government that persisted in investigating the human rights abuses of the armed forces during the Dirty War. In a concerted counter-attack involving the illegal use of white phosphorous, the AMLs fired on the militants contributing to their total annihilation. La Guerra Sucia remains a cancer in the heart of Argentine society to this day.

Israel

The AML unit named Duchifat came about because, to the crews, the front shape of the AML resembled the beak of a Duchifat or Hoopoe bird that subsequently became the national bird of Israel in 2004. The unit was established following a visit to France by the head of the IDF Paratroop and Infantry Corps – Col Aharon Davidi. There he witnessed a presentation of the AML 90 together with the SA 321K Super Frelon heavy-lift helicopter. The latter was capable of lifting a single AML as was demonstrated by the French to Col Davidi. This capability fulfilled a requirement by the IDF 35th Paratroop Brigade for armour and fire support on deep-penetration raids inside Arab territory. In consequence, the IDF immediately ordered 14 AML 90s and six Super Frelon helicopters. The latter were delivered on 20 April 1966 with the inauguration of 114 Squadron operating out of Tel Nof air base.

However, further trials of the AML and Super Frelon combination showed that the helicopter was incapable of lifting a fully armed and crewed AML 90, particularly in the hot conditions prevalent in the Middle East. It transpires that the French used an unladen AML without crew, fuel or ammunition in the demonstration for Col Davidi. In consequence, Duchifat became one of the ground reconnaissance elements within the 35th Paratroop Brigade with the designation Unit 70 as Duchifat was never an official designation.

CENTRE AND LEFT The purchase of the AML 90 by the IDF was predicated on it being able to be flown by a Super Frelon helicopter or a Transall C-160 transport aircraft, but the French demonstration was somewhat suspect in that the vehicle carried no ammunition, crew or fuel, with even the commander's hatch removed and the tyres deflated.

Established in November 1966, the AML company was divided into three platoons of four vehicles and two in a headquarters section, with one for the commanding officer and one for his second in command. The first commander was an outstanding young paratrooper officer, Lt Ehud Shani, who was deemed destined for the highest of commands within the IDF. In early 1967 the unit began intensive training at the Armour School at Julis base camp in southern Israel. The crews undertook several courses to allow them to perform each other's duties within the AML and they had almost finished their training by the outbreak of the Six-Day War on 5 June. At the outset, there was no particular role for Unit 70 since much of the 35th Paratroop Brigade was deployed to the Sinai, so Lt Shani immediately approached Army Headquarters and demanded an assignment for the AMLs.

In the event, Unit 70 was posted to Central Command for the offensive into the West Bank and the supreme prize – Jerusalem. Two platoons of nine armoured cars, an infantry platoon and maintenance personnel in half-tracks under the command of Ehud Shani came under the command of the 10th 'Harel' Armoured Brigade whose task was to encircle Jerusalem from the north and prevent the Jordanians from reinforcing their forces in the city. The other AML platoon of five vehicles under the command of the unit's deputy commander, Lt Yoram Kafri, was assigned to

ABOVE The AML 90s of Unit 70 of the 35th Paratroop Brigade undergo exercises in the Negev Desert shortly before the outbreak of the Six-Day War in June 1967.

the 'Kiryati' Brigade that was initially responsible for the defence of central Israel, but later was tasked with the conquest of Latrun and then take the offensive eastwards towards Ramallah. The former fortress of Latrun was heavily disputed and denied to the IDF during the War of Independence in 1948 so its early capture was especially satisfying. It subsequently became the headquarters of the Israeli Armoured Corps.

BELOW A Duchifat AML 90 of the 'Kiryati' Brigade moves out of the Palestinian village of Beit Hanina on the road to Ramallah on 7 June 1967.

On the morning of 6 June, after a night of sporadic fighting, the commander of the 10th Brigade, Col Uri Ben-Ari, tasked the 106th Battalion with Duchifat in the lead since most of the brigade's armoured companies were equipped to advance eastwards with elderly Shermans that suffered mechanically in the steep Judean hills. Immediately on receiving their orders to move as fast as possible to the Hizma junction and prevent the Jordanian 60th Armoured Brigade from crossing it, the Duchifat AML 90s advanced from Biddu to Har Shmuel. After a short fight at the Tomb of Samuel, the unit advanced to Beit Hanina and on towards Shuafat: an exclusive village for wealthy Palestinians from Ramallah and Jerusalem. At the same time, the Jordanian 60th Armoured Brigade was moving towards Jerusalem from Jericho. The brigade was equipped with M48 Pattons, which were considered to be the best tanks in service with the Jordanian Army. Fouga CM-170 Magister jets of the Israeli Air Force tried and failed to stop the Jordanian brigade that now arrived at the village of Hizma where the tanks were dug in to reduce the effects of air attack.

Around 10.00hrs, the leading Duchifat armoured cars were descending from the Shuafat ridge on an ancient road that was little more than a track when they came under mortar and direct tank fire. Lt Shani ordered his deputy, Lt Gidi, to move his platoon and take up covering fire positions on a small nearby hill, Tel Aful, while the remaining five vehicles continued the advance eastwards still under fire. Within moments, the AML 90 of Ehud Shani was hit in the turret by a 90mm shell, killing him and his gunner instantly while the driver escaped without serious injury. By now the positions of the dug-in Pattons were visible due to the dust and debris thrown up on firing. A companion AML 90 identified and engaged a Patton at short range, striking it in the turret whereupon the tank burst into flames. Meanwhile, Gidi's armoured cars were now in their firing positions but also under fire from Jeep-mounted 106mm recoilless rifles.

Inside one of the AMLs was Tsur Bunim acting as gunner:

'I observed across the valley in front of us three or maybe four Patton tanks firing regularly. Yael the commander of our AML gave me the direction and I laid the cross hairs on the target at a range of between 800 and 1,000m and then fired. We saw the hit and the explosion followed by fire and the crew jumping out of the Patton. The commander then told the driver to roll back and get us into dead ground so I could reload the gun. He was an excellent driver and

BELOW A pair of Duchifat AML 90s manoeuvre on the skyline in a manner reminiscent of the action at Tel El-Ful on 6 June 1967 against the Jordanian 60th Armoured Brigade.

LEFT The remaining AML 90s of Duchifat take part in the victory parade held at Rafah soon after the Six-Day War. Note the painted white 'T' on the turret roof that was an air recognition device during the war.

we were soon under cover. Once reloaded we moved up to the crest where Yael indicated another tank to the right of the burning one. Again I laid the cross hairs on the target and BOOM the same result. But then Gidi called on the radio to say one of our AMLs had been hit. I immediately opened my hatch and looked out and saw the AML next to me on fire with the ammunition exploding. Once again we lost two guys, the commander and gunner. Yael then fired our smoke grenades and the top of the hill was suddenly covered by thick smoke to allow the remaining vehicles to withdraw to the bottom of the hill. It was there that we heard that Ehud Shani had been hit. I have to say we were most upset by the lack of air force cover that left us fighting 45-ton tanks in 5-ton armoured cars. Of course it was just as we were driving back to Shafat that the air force began to attack the enemy.'

After suffering losses of several tanks, the Jordanian brigade stopped firing and their soldiers started to abandon their tanks and run away. This was a battle that neutralised the main Jordanian armoured force intended to reinforce the troops fighting inside Jerusalem: a brigade of tanks stymied by just nine AML 90s whose combined weight was less than that of one M48 Patton.

Needless to say the glory went to the paratroopers of Col Motta Gur's reserve paratrooper brigade that conquered Jerusalem and the Old City in the defining action of the Six-Day War.

Operation 'Inferno' – the Battle of Karameh

On 21 March 1968, Duchifat participated in the ill-fated Battle of Karameh against elements of the Palestine Liberation Organisation (PLO) within Jordan. The goal of the battle was to destroy the infrastructure of the PLO that had moved its bases to Jordan and stepped up their attacks inside Israel. Under the command of the 35th Paratrooper Brigade, Duchifat was again divided into two parts for Operation 'Inferno'. The main one comprised two platoons under the company commander, Lt Amnon Lipkin-Shahak. It joined the northern force under the command of Gen Rafael 'Raful' Eitan that crossed the Jordan river via the Damia bridge. The role of this force was to stop PLO fighters from escaping Karameh, as well as to prevent the intervention of any Jordanian forces during the incursion. The second part consisted of one platoon under Duchifat deputy commander, Lt Gidi Ben Yosef, which joined the raiding force of the legendary paratrooper Danny Matt. The overall purpose of Operation 'Inferno' was the destruction of the headquarters of the PLO in Karameh, including the PLO's leader, Yasser Arafat, whom intelligence indicated was located there.

The IDF's actions on both incursion routes faced many difficulties both from the terrain and the explicit orders not to avoid Jordanian civilian casualties. In the south, most of the PLO fighters succeeded in escaping to the north via the Jordanian side of the Jordan Rift

Valley thanks to prior intelligence of the IDF raid, including of course Yasser Arafat. In the north, the Israeli armoured force was halted almost immediately after crossing the Jordan river due to flooding of the area following the destruction of irrigation ditches by the Jordanians.

Thereafter the Israeli force was attacked by accurate Jordanian artillery and tank fire. To continue with the mission, Rafael Eitan ordered Duchifat armoured cars to join the tanks and move towards a junction that was controlled by well-camouflaged and dug-in Jordanian tanks. This attack did not go well and Israeli forces suffered significant loses. Two armoured cars and several tanks were hit. Four Duchifat crewmen were killed and an additional two were wounded. The armoured cars found themselves under Jordanian crossfire in waterlogged terrain in which they could not manoeuvre freely, fighting an eight-hour battle against superior forces. Inevitably the evacuation of casualties under fire became the priority, supervised by the gallant Lt Lipkin-Shahak. He was subsequently awarded the first of two Medals of Courage, Israel's second highest decoration for bravery, during his illustrious career that culminated in him becoming the fifteenth IDF Chief of Staff, a position that many thought would have been achieved by Lt Ehud Shani the original commander of Duchifat. The unit was disbanded soon after the Battle of Karameh, which remains a significant defeat for the IDF.

BELOW A trio of Eland Mk 5 armoured cars of the Rhodesian Armoured Car Regiment display the typical camouflage scheme of the Bush War with green stripes over the base neutral colour and the spare wheel moved to the turret roof to allow easier escape through the side door.

Rhodesia

The Rhodesian Bush War lasted from 1964 to 1979 at a time when wars of liberation were prevalent across black Africa. Spurned by the British in 1965, Rhodesia was subject to a United Nations arms embargo with just Portugal and South Africa as a conduit for modern weapons. At the outbreak of hostilities against the guerilla groups of ZANLA and ZIPRA based in Zambia and Mozambique, the Rhodesian Security Forces were largely equipped with British weapons: some dating back to the Second World War such as the Staghound Mk 1 armoured car. Twenty of these served into the 1960s with the Support Group of 1 Light Infantry until the time of the Unilateral Declaration of Independence when they were moved to Kariba for border defence. On the actual day of UDI, 11 November 1965, one Staghound fired a symbolic 2pdr (37mm) round into Zambia.

First formed in 1941, the Rhodesian Armoured Car Regiment (Rh ACR) was re-established in 1972 under the command of Maj Bruce Rooken-Smith. The main AFV used by the regiment was the Ferret Mk 2 armoured car. The vehicle was affectionately known as 'George' but again just 20 of them served in the Bush War. Acquired from the British Army's Middle East Command in 1960, the Ferrets were elderly even before their arrival in Rhodesia. Nevertheless, the standard of

maintenance was very high and the Ferrets were repeatedly overhauled, incorporating several local modifications such as enlarged fuel tanks. One was even fitted with a new turret mounting a 20mm cannon that proved too powerful for the turret ring to absorb. Furthermore, the arrival of the first 16 Eland 90 Mk 5s in 1975 onwards obviated the need for such radical modification. Initially, the clutch on these vehicles proved problematical, especially when driving in the hilly Eastern Highlands where engine overheating was also prevalent. The clutch problem was solved by fitting modified Land Rover units. In 1979, the regiment began to receive Eland Mk 6s to give a grand total of some 60 vehicles.

ABOVE Throughout the Bush and Border Wars of the 1970s, both Rhodesia and South Africa developed a whole gamut of armoured vehicles to protect against the principal threat of mines. This Albatross Mechanical Horse was developed to deliver mine-protected vehicles to the front and return with damaged ones. It is seen here transporting three Eland 90s to Rhodesia.

The regiment was based at Blakiston-Houston Barracks in Salisbury and consisted of four Armoured Car Squadrons with A, B and C Squadrons manned by Territorials and D by Regulars and National Servicemen. Each squadron comprised four troops of four vehicles, often a mix of Elands and Ferrets. Finally, E Squadron was formed in October 1979 with eight T-55 tanks that had been

BELOW A C47 Dakota comes in to land at FAF1 with a diminutive Eland 60 guarding the airstrip. *(Mark Richardson)*

RIGHT A 'pirated' T-55TD of E Squadron rests in the background behind the principal AFV of the Rhodesian Armoured Car Regiment during the Bush War. Like their South African counterparts, a decision was taken not to provide a gun shield at the commander's position since they then became a bigger target tor RPG anti-armour weapons, whereas the average enemy soldier was a notoriously poor marksman.

destined for Idi Amin's regime in Uganda as a gift of Col Qaddafi. The French ship *Astor* sailing from Libya docked at Durban in South Africa and the ten Polish-built T-55TDs on board were seized by the authorities. Two went to the SAAC School of Armour at Bloemfontein for evaluation and the remainder to Rhodesia. Commanded by a former Bundeswehr officer Capt Heinz Kaufeldt, the T-55 tanks did not see action during the Bush War although they were a central facet of Operation 'Quartz', the proposed assassination of Robert Mugabe and the ZANU leadership on 4 March 1980.

During the war, Rhodesia was divided into seven operational areas, each with suitably bellicose names such as Grapple, Repulse and Thrasher. D Squadron was deployed for much of the Bush War with a troop of Eland 90s at Victoria Falls, Umtali and Kariba, with a troop of Ferrets at Chipinga. The Territorial squadrons were originally tasked to support the six Independent Companies of the Rhodesia Regiment, based at Wankie, Kariba, Inyanga and Umtali, but in practice they were employed wherever needed. These Independent Companies formed the basis of all arms teams comprising infantry, artillery, helicopters, paratroopers and AFVs. These were often employed for cross-border raids into Zambia and Mozambique.

For many of the tasks of counter-insurgency operations, the Ferret proved to be more than adequate, but armed with just a single Browning 7.62mm machine-gun it lacked the firepower to provide effective support to

BELOW Throughout the Bush War, the Rhodesian armed forces employed all manner of weapons and vehicles with the most important shown here: an Eland Mk 5 in the background, the Crocodile improvised APC at left, and the ubiquitous Unimog 406 that was used for a host of purposes from cargo carrier to command vehicle and from ambulance to recoilless rifle platform (as here).

the infantry in a serious firefight. Accordingly, over time, some 60 Eland 90s were acquired from South Africa on loan, together with 10 Eland 60s that equipped the Rhodesian Air Force Regiment for forward airfield defence and the escort of aviation fuel convoys. To maintain some semblance of deniability, the original Elands carried SAP (South African Police) registration plates. Besides counter-insurgency duties, the regiment prepared for more conventional warfare against the possibility of invasion from the terrorist bases in neighbouring Zambia and Mozambique where the local insurgency group FRELIMO were known to have T-34/85 and T54 tanks as well as other Soviet supplied AFVs such as the BTR-152. Some of the latter were encountered at Entumbane 2 in 1981 and disintegrated under the firepower of the Elands' 90mm guns. In the words of Maj Rooken-Smith: 'It was like shooting pheasants on the ground.'

Despite a South African stipulation that the Elands were not to be used on external raids, this was routinely ignored and they were employed as the situation dictated. During Operation 'Miracle', they spearheaded the assault on 'Monte Cassino', a heavily defended hilltop ZANLA complex at New Chimoio. A counter-attack by FRELIMO tanks caused some anxiety, but the Rhodesians were able to disperse them with 25pdr guns and two Hawker

ABOVE **With the coming of independence, all the AML 60s of the Rhodesian Air Force Regiment were returned to South Africa as were most of the AML 90s of the Rhodesian Armoured Car Regiment.**

Hunter jets without committing their armoured cars. Trooper Dave Hughes recalls the operation:

'I was the gunner on Eland 90 call sign Four Two Alpha during Operation "Miracle" in September–October 1979. The guns and all vehicles were painted Frelimo "green" for the raid. During the battle which lasted five days and four nights the Rhodesian "arty" of 25pdrs was instrumental in driving back a Frelimo armoured column consisting of a half-dozen T-54s and several BTR152 APCs that attacked the raiders during the third or fourth nights of the operation. The next morning our Eland 90s 42, 42A and 42B along with Capt Winkler's Unimog mounting twin .30-cal machine-guns loaded with AP and API ammo followed up the tracks of the retreating Frelimo column with the help of a Lynx aircraft mounting machine-guns and rocket launchers until the enemy bomb-shelled (dispersed) and we were ordered to break off the chase by the operation commanders circling overhead in the command Dakota aircraft.'

It was the last external raid of the war. Throughout the war the regiment suffered relatively few casualties because the enemy

ABOVE This particular AML 60 sports a variation of the famous Desert Rats symbol with AFV at the top and the legend 'SEEK & SQUEAK' at the bottom, a jibe directed at No 4 Squadron whose motto was 'Seek and Strike'. *(Mark Richardson)*

BELOW Following independence, the Zimbabwean Army was reduced to a single armoured car squadron of 12 AML 90s divided into four platoons, each with a UR-416 M armoured personnel carrier.

tended to avoid contact with the Elands as far as possible. The principal reason for this was the devastating effect of the shells from the Eland's 90mm gun. Landmines caused the majority of casualties. Following the creation of Zimbabwe, some 16 Eland 90s remained in service that were integrated into a single squadron. Plans were laid to upgrade the vehicles with the Panhard 90mm Lynx turret but they came to naught. Most if not all were lost in Mugabe's disastrous intervention in the Second Congo War of 1998.

AML Senegal

The armed forces of Senegal (Forces Armées du Sénégal) acquired 74 AML 90s and 30 AML 60s. A large number of these were provided by Saudi Arabia as a token of appreciation of Senegal's contribution to the Coalition Forces in the Gulf War of 1991. Tragically, the Senegal contingent of 500 men suffered disastrous casualties when a plane crash killed 92 of them on 21 March 1991 soon after the end of the war.

ABOVE A line-up of Panhard AML 90s of the Saudi Arabian Army after Operation 'Desert Storm' prior to them being given to Niger and Senegal. Note that these vehicles are fitted with infrared night-fighting equipment.

LEFT These brand new AML 90s are part of the first consignment to be delivered to Senegal in 1976. The AMLs are attached to the 22nd, 24th and 25th Armoured Battalions and to the 26ème Bataillon de Reconnaissance et d'Appui.

ABOVE This AML 90 is named 'KOSSOU' after the largest lake in the country and was delivered in 1976 as the armed forces of the Ivory Coast expanded to meet the threat of civil war.

south as well as mutinies to bolster or remove incumbent presidents: a role well suited to the ubiquitous AML.

AML Yemen

Following the Yemenite War of 1979, North Yemen received a quantity of AML 90s and 60s from Saudi Arabia to make up for losses of AFVs during the conflict between North and South Yemen. Since both sides were copiously equipped with Soviet material, the AML 60s were modified to take the 14.5mm KPVT heavy machine-gun turrets from BTR-60PB armoured personnel vehicles. Conversely, the turret of the AML 90s was married with the hull of the BTR for greater fire support to the infantry. A similar modification was undertaken in Djibouti as well.

AML Ivory Coast

The army of the Ivory Coast was originally equipped with ex-French Army M8 Greyhound armoured cars but these were superseded by 20 AML 90s in 1968 and subsequently 16 Panhard M3 APCs. Typical of several West African countries, the Ivory Coast has endured continuing civil strife between the predominantly Muslim north and the Christian

AML and Eland, Gabon

The armed forces of Gabon acquired 31 AML 60s and 90s between 1968 and 1983. These vehicles equipped the 1st Light Armoured Reconnaissance Squadron of the Republican Guard Battalion whose main task was the protection of the eccentric and corrupt President El Hadj Omar Bongo who ruled Gabon from 1967 until his death in

BELOW AML 90s and modified AML 60s of the Republican Guard take part in a parade in the Yemen capital of Sana'a.

Gabon was just one of several African countries to procure clandestine consignments of Elands from South Africa despite African Union sanctions against the latter.

2009. As leader of the Gabon Democratic Party, he gained 99.56% of the votes cast in the presidential elections of 1973 only to be surpassed at 99.97% of the popular vote in 1985. His presidential palace in the capital Libreville had two AML 90s permanently manned and positioned as gate guards but without engines. Polished to perfection and with white wall tyres, the AMLs had their guns trained at 90° towards each other and the crews were required to rotate the turrets to the front whenever the gates were opened. After serious rioting in May 1990 against his autocratic rule, President Bongo was only maintained in power thanks to the commitment of Foreign Legion paratroopers with Operation 'Requin' – 'to protect the interests of 20,000 French nationals'. Many of the Gabonese tanks and armoured cars sent to protect the presidential palace failed to arrive because of mechanical failure. Accordingly, President Bongo turned to South Africa for help, despite the African Union embargo on dealings with

the country. Under the codename Operation 'Sexton', unmarked Safair Lockheed L-100-20 Hercules aircraft flew four Eland 90s and four Eland 60s with a training team directly to Libreville to bolster the Presidential Guard. In 2018, 24 AMLs and Elands remain in service but are being superseded by Nexter Systems Aravis Multipurpose Heavily Protected Armoured Vehicles.

AML Kenya

A troop of Kenyan AML Lynx armoured cars pauses at Liboi on the Somali border prior to undertaking Operation 'Linda Nchi' (or

BELOW A troop of Kenyan AML Lynx armoured cars pauses at Liboi on the Somali border prior to undertaking Operation 'Linda Nchi' or 'Protect our Country' to combat Al-Shabab terrorists inside Somalia.

ABOVE On 28 September 2012, Kenyan AMISOM forces and troops of the Somali National Army launched a combined land and amphibious assault against the port of Kismayo, the last major city controlled by Al-Shabab and source of much of their funds. During an Al-Shabab attack against Kenyan positions at Kismayo airport, these Kenyan AMLs killed seven terrorists after engaging their technical, which is seen here being dragged back to the airport. These AMLs carry the letters 'AU' on the turret sides to denote African Union.

'Protect our Country') to combat Al-Shabab terrorists inside Somalia.

The Kenyan Army has been a long-term user of the Panhard AML armoured car with both 90s and 60s. A total of 72 were procured and these have been modernised in part to the AML Lynx version. The country of Somalia has been devastated by war for decades, whether in fighting Ethiopia, repeated civil wars, Al-Qaeda Horn of Africa and, latterly, its latest manifestation of Al-Shabab. The latter has made repeated attacks against Kenyan interests and citizens from its bases in southern Somalia, as well as kidnapping foreign nationals such as aid workers. In retaliation, the Kenyan Defence Forces launched Operation 'Linda Nchi' on 16 October 2011 with some 4,200 troops to eradicate Al-Shabab bases across southern

Somalia to the Indian Ocean. The campaign continued until March 2012 and thereafter Kenyan forces came under the African Union peacekeeping operation AMISOM (African Union Mission In Somalia) under the aegis of the United Nations that continues at the time of writing (2018) to contain Al-Shabab.

AML Lynx Niger

The Niger Army procured a total of 88 AML 90s and a mixture of 35 AML 20s and 60s over a period of a decade from 1983 to 1992. In addition it purchased seven Panhard VBLs or Véhicule Blindé Léger as shown here to the left of the baobab tree. The latter is also known as a 'palaver tree' where Africans congregate under its shade to converse and settle disputes, or even as a setting for story-telling and entertainment. The Panhards are divided into four armoured reconnaissance squadrons that are employed mostly to interdict the smuggling of weapons from the failed state of Libya to AQIM and Boko Haram terrorist groups. They are also used in the ongoing low-level insurgency by Taureg and Tobou rebels in the northern and eastern deserts of the country.

AML Mauritania

As of 2007 the Mauritanian Army possessed 35 T-54/55 battle tanks and 60 Panhard AFVs including 40 AML 90s, 20 AML 60s and 20 M3 VTT armoured personnel carriers. As two former French colonies, Mauritania and Senegal fought a Border War between 1989 and 1991 over grazing and water rights. As both countries were equipped with AML armoured cars, it held the curious prospect of such vehicles fighting each other.

ABOVE Two AML 90 Lynx armoured cars and a Panhard VBL pause during a patrol in the eastern region of Niger.

LEFT AML 90s take part in the Mauritania Independence Day celebrations on 28 November 2009.

AML Djibouti

Djibouti is located in the Aden Gulf at one of the most strategically important and volatile areas in the world, including the Bab-el-Mandeb strait into the Red Sea through which much commercial shipping flows and is an area of long-standing piracy. The armed forces of Djibouti procured 24 AML 60s and 90s in 1979 to equip the reconnaissance squadron of an armoured regiment that comprises three armoured squadrons and an anti-smuggling squadron. These vehicles were employed in the Djiboutian Civil War between 1991 and 2001 and during numerous border clashes with Eritrea over the Ras Doumeira peninsula. The fiercest of these occurred on 10–13 June 2008 in which 44 Djiboutian soldiers were killed and 55 wounded as against 100 Eritrean dead and 121 captured. The dispute remains unresolved to this day.

AML Iraq

The Iraqi army was a major user of the AML with a total of 357 60s and 90s as well as 115 M3 VTT in various versions. Several AML 90s were employed with little success during the Battle of Khafji from 29 January to 1 February 1991. As part of the subterfuge (picture left) the vehicles were adorned with the inverted V mutual recognition markings of the Coalition Forces. The attack into Saudi Arabia by the Iraqi Third Corps was repulsed with heavy losses.

AML El Salvador

El Salvador is the smallest country on the American continent. It is also the most densely populated and that has been the cause of much of its misery over the years. Once the sole source of commercial indigo, it then became totally dependent on the export of coffee: a business controlled by a corrupt oligarchy known as 'las catorce families' or 'Fourteen Families' in collusion with a military dictatorship that was supported by the United

BELOW With FAES displayed on the side of the turret denoting Fuerza Armada de El Salvador, an AML 90 stands guard on a highway in central El Salvador on 1 June 1983. At that time the armed forces of El Salvador were killing hundreds of civilians a month in a civil war of the utmost barbarity, with an ultimate death toll of over 70,000 in 12 years of warfare – 85% of them killed by government forces and their notorious Death Squads. (/Getty Images)

RIGHT Displaying a distinctive digital camouflage system, this FAES AML 90 has been modernised with a Peugeot XD 3T liquid-cooled diesel engine, seen here with modified air intake cowlings.

BELOW An Eland Mk 7 belonging to the Chadian contingent of FOMAC (Multinational Force for Central Africa) undertakes a patrol during the Central Africa Republic Civil War to separate the rebels of the Séléka coalition and the Anti-Balaka militia during 2014.

States. Following the disastrous 'Soccer War' with Honduras in July 1969, opposition to the autocratic government grew during the 1970s with multiple left-wing factions engaged in uncoordinated guerilla warfare. Following several civilian massacres and the murder of

the outspoken and popular Archbishop Óscar Romero, the multifarious guerilla groups joined forces to form the Frente Farabundo Martí de Liberacion Nacional (FMLN) in October 1980. Three months later, the Salvadorean Civil War began in earnest when the FMLN

launched a countrywide offensive. At the time, the Cavalry Regiment of the Fuerza Armada de El Salvador (FAES) was equipped with 12 Panhard AML H90 armoured cars. They were first used operationally in January 1981 when the garrison in Santa Ana city was overrun by the FMLN. Santa Anna was once the most prosperous city in El Salvador during the 'golden age of coffee'. All 12 Panhards of the Cavalry Regiment were quickly deployed to the beleaguered city and recaptured the army barracks within 24 hours. Thereafter the armoured cars were employed in the fire support role and for road escort duties. One H90 was destroyed by an RPG during an action near Guazapa and a second was lost in Usulatan in a conflagration after striking an anti-personnel mine. In the harsh tropical conditions of El Salvador, the Model 4 HD gasoline engine broke down frequently due to overheating and spare parts were rapidly consumed. By the mid-1980s, several Panhards had been cannibalised to keep the others in running condition. At the end of the war in January 1992, the Cavalry Regiment was reduced to six operational Panhard AML H90s.

AML FOMAC

In a truly awful conflict in which almost a quarter of the population has been displaced, the mainly Muslim Séléka and Christian Anti-Balaka forces have committed utterly unspeakable war crimes against each other and both have terrorised civilians in yet another tragic instance of genocide. In the Central African Republic, the term 'laka' denotes the AK-47 Kalashnikov assault rifle, thus Anti-Balaka means 'anti laka (AK-47) bullets' but only if the militiaman or child soldier is wearing a 'grigri'. This is a Voodoo amulet which protects the wearer from evil spirits and M43 7.62mm x 39mm rounds, as well as acting as a method of birth control. The vehicle is flying the flags of Chad and insignia of FOMAC on its front.

AML Beirut 1983

On 23 October 1983, two suicide truck bombs were detonated beside buildings housing members of the Multinational Force in Lebanon killing 241 US and 58 French peacekeepers. The latter were paratroopers of the 1er and

BELOW Here, an RICM AML 90 is liberally adorned with tricolors and, most unusually for French AMLs, the vehicle is fitted with a roof-mounted 7.5mm AA-52 machine-gun.

FOREIGN SALES OF AMLs AND M3 APCs

Overseas sales of the Panhard AML series were considerable from a total output of 6,035 vehicles as of 1994 and a further 1,300 produced in South Africa. Any list of foreign sales can only be partial, but it gives an indication of the diversity of countries that have employed the AML series.

Abu-Dhabi	106 x AML 90 F1
Algeria	54 x AML 60 CS
Argentina	60 x AML 90 F1
Bahrein	22 x AML 90 F1
Burkina Faso	4 x AML 90 F1
Burundi	15 x AML 60 CS + 6 x AML 60 HB
Cambodia	2 x AML 60 CS
Côte D'Ivoire	10 x AML 60 CS + 6 x AML 90 F1
Djibouti	1 x AML 60 HB + 7 x AML 90 F1
Ecuador	12 x AML 60 CS + 15 x AML 90 F1
El Salvador	12x AML 90 F1
Ethiopia	56 x AML 60 CS
Gabon	3 x AML 60 CS + 4 x AML 60 HB + 2 x AML 60/20 + 8 x AML 90 F1
Iraq	128 x AML 60/20 + 101 x AML 90 F1
Ireland	16 x AML 60 CS + 16 x AML 60 HB + 20 x AML 90 F1
Israel	14 x AML 90 F1 (modified gun)
Kenya	8 x AML 60 CS + 22 x AML 60/20 + 38 x AML 90 F1
Lebanon	52 x AML 90 F1 + 43 x AML 90 Lynx
Mauritania	19 x AML 60 CS + 5 x AML 60 HB +15 x AML 60/20 +14 x AML 90 F1
Morocco	20 x AML 60 HB + 176 x AML 90 F1 + 6 x AML 90 Lynx
Niger	6 x AML 60 CS + 2 x AML 60/20 + 16 x AML 90 F1 + 10 x AML 60 Serval
Nigeria	7 x AML 60 CS + 124 AML 60 HB + 12 x AML 90 F1
Pakistan	5 x AML 60/20
Portugal	28 x AML 60/CS
Rwanda	12 x AML 60 CS + 15 x AML 60 HB
Saudi Arabia	83 x AML 60 CS + 167 AML 90 F1 + 2 AML École de Pilotage
Senegal	30 x AML 60 CS + 24 x AML 90 F1
South Africa	100 x AML 60 CS
Spain	103 x AML 60 CS + 100 x AML 90 F1
Sudan	6 x AML 90 F1
Tchad	10 x AML 60 CS + 8 x AML 90 F1 + 11 x AML 90 Lynx
Togo	3 x AML 60 CS + 7 x AML 90 F1
Tunisia	33 x AML 90 F1
Yemen	146 x AML 90 F1
Zaire	135 x AML 60 CS + 47 x AML 90 F1

Sales of the M3 to the following countries:	
Algeria	44 VTT, 5 VPC, 2 VAT, 2 VLA, 2 VTS
Angola	8 VTT
Bahrain	3 VTS, 8 PC, 3 VLA, 87 VTT, 5 VAT, 7 PM81
Burkina Faso	1 PC, 17 VTT, 1 VAT
Burundi	9 VTT
Chad	15 VTT
Congo	9 VTT
Democratic Republic of Congo	86, including 60 VTT
Gabon	2 PC, 4 VTT, 1 VAT
Iraq	161 VTT
Ireland	60 VTT
Ivory Coast	4 VPC, 10 VTT, 2 VAT, 6 VDA
Kenya	3 VPC, 3 VTT, 6 VAT
Lebanon	57 VTT
Malaysia	44 VTT
Mauritania	4 VPC, 4 VTT, 4 VAT
Morocco	4 VPC, 36 VTT, 14 VAT
Niger	4 PC, 12 VTT, 10 VDA
Nigeria	4 VTS, 6 VPC, 4 VSB (RASIT), 4 VAT
Paraguay	3 VTT
Portugal	6 VTT
Rwanda	16 VTT
Saudi Arabia	5 VPC, 165 VTT
Senegal	1 PC, 9 VTT
Somali Republic	9 VTT
Spain	23 VTT
Sudan	13 VTT, 1 VAT, 2 VSB (RASIT), 2 VSB (RA 20)
Togo	5 VTT
Tunisia	24 VTT
United Arab Emirates	13 VTS, 30 PC, 150 VTT, 5 VAT, 48 VDA
Venezuela	4 VTT
Yemen	2 VTT

9ème Parachute Chasseur Régiments. The Residence des Pins or French Embassy Residence was attacked by various armed groups and the ambassador killed. To prevent further acts of terrorism, the armoured cars of the Régiment d'Infanterie-Chars de Marine (RICM) were deployed to protect the residence and embassy grounds.

AML FNLA

Following the Portuguese withdrawal from Angola, various communist factions sought to impose themselves as the legitimate government, including the People's Movement for the Liberation of Angola or MPLA and the National Liberation Front of Angola or FNLA. President Mobutu Sese Seko of Zaire wished for a pro-Kinshasa regime in Angola so gave significant military aid to the FNLA under Holden Roberto before independence was declared. Comprising some 1,200 Zairian troops and

several AML armoured cars in support of 2,000 FNLA fighters, this force marched on Luanda, the capital of Angola, from the north-west, defeating the MPLA at Porto Quipiri. Despite vehement protests from South Africa advisers, Holden Roberto launched an ill-advised assault on Luanda on 10 November, the day before independence. At the battle of Quifangondo, the FNLA, together with the Zairian troops, were comprehensively defeated by artillery and rocket fire from BM-21 multiple rocket launchers manned by Cubans. During the battle, the Panhard armoured cars were manned by Portuguese former commandos acting as mercenaries under the command of Col Santos e Castro. They suffered significant casualties due to the heavy artillery bombardment and withdrew in disarray.

BELOW Zairian Panhard armoured cars with the letters 'FNLA' stencilled on the turret sides stand by before the Battle of Quifangondo.

Chapter Seven

Eland in combat

The Eland entered combat in a role for which it was never intended. Throughout Operation 'Savannah' in Angola during late 1975, the Eland armoured car acted as a light tank and proved highly successful in battle. Accordingly, this account concentrates exclusively on the Eland's exploits during 'Savannah' despite the fact that it continued to give sterling service in many subsequent operations of the Border War.

OPPOSITE The Eland Mk 7 90 was the final and definitive model to be produced for the South African Army as well as for export. Introduced in 1978, production continued until 1986 when the Eland was about to be superseded by the formidable 8 x 8 Rooikat armoured car.

LEFT The Border War began in 1966 but by 1974 it was necessary to deploy the army in support of the police conducting the counter-insurgency campaign in South West Africa. Here, a pair of Eland 60s conducts a patrol in the eastern Caprivi Strip that, due to its geography, was prone to infiltration by SWAPO.

Operation 'Savannah'

The Portuguese withdrawal from Angola following the Carnation Revolution of April 1974 precipitated the breakdown of law and order in the country as hundreds of thousands of people fled their homes to seek safety in one of the largest civil migrations ever in peacetime. Anarchy ensued as an alphabet soup of warring groups fought each other to gain supremacy before the handover of government that was scheduled for 11 November 1975. Each faction was of a communist persuasion, from Marxists to Maoists, with FAPLA, FNLA, MPLA, PLAN, SWAPO, UNITA et al, vying for power through the barrel of a gun, invariably a Kalashnikov, in a bitter civil war. In the spring of 1975, the Soviet Union, together with its Cuban acolytes, threw their support behind the MPLA with a massive influx of war materiel and combat advisers with the outset of Opéracion 'Carlota'. Between March and November 1975 the Soviets sent a total of 27 shiploads and some 40 cargo planes of weaponry to the MPLA and its surrogate insurgent arm, FAPLA.

In response, US President Gerald Ford authorised the CIA on 18 July 1975 to undertake Operation '1A Feature'. This was intended to provide backing to the FNLA and UNITA as a countermeasure since southern Africa was now of vital strategic importance in the ongoing Cold War. Following the closure of the Suez Canal because of the October War of 1973, western oil supplies now had to pass the Cape of Good Hope and were thus vulnerable to Soviet forces based in Angola if the Marxist–Leninist MPLA came to power – as were the oil and mineral wealth of the country itself.

The Western powers, together with several African countries such as Zaire and Zambia, now persuaded the government of South Africa

RIGHT The original role for the Eland in the early 1960s was as an urban, rural and border patrol vehicle. It was never considered as an offensive AFV or tank substitute that it became during and after Operation 'Savannah' in 1975. But such was the Elands' success that the enemy dubbed them the 'Red Ants' for their ability to be everywhere and deliver a fierce bite.

to intervene in Angola to restore stability. On 9 August 1975, troops of the South African Defence Force (SADF) deployed a platoon of infantry and a pair of Eland armoured cars to guard the vital hydroelectric complex at Ruacana, as well as the Calueque barrage some 25 miles up-river inside Angola, which supplied power to much of South West Africa. Other forces provided security against SWAPO insurgents infiltrating South West Africa from their bases in southern Angola in a conflict that had been waging since 1966. On 21 August, armoured cars of D Squadron, 2 Special Service Battalion (SSB) attached to 2 South African Infantry Regiment based at Ondangwa supported a paratrooper incursion into Angola with their H60 mortars when a firefight between MPLA and UNITA forces threatened to spill over the border. With its new-found wealth of military hardware, the MPLA was expanding its influence from the coastal region northwards against the FNLA and eastwards against UNITA, threatening the latter's headquarters in Nova Lisboa. By the end of August 1975, the MPLA was in control of 11 of the 16 district capitals of Angola. From September, the SADF provided both FNLA and UNITA with military advisers while the CIA covertly delivered weapons via Zaire. Operation 'Savannah' was officially launched on 3 September 1975.

RIGHT The first tank supplied to the Angolans and Cubans was the venerable T-34/85. Invariably it was employed in a static role as mobile artillery in dug-in positions, as seen here. Although capable of destroying an Eland with a single shot, it more often than not fell victim to the superior training and handling of the Eland 90 crews. The T-34/85 was first encountered during Operation 'Savannah'.

At the time, UNITA possessed just four battle-weary Panhard armoured cars provided by Zaire. Using components from one, three of these, two H90s, and one H60, were made serviceable by six members from the Technical Service Corps of the SADF flown in to provide mechanical expertise between 26 and 30 September. They also gave just three days of instruction to the UNITA crews before they were committed to battle early in October. In the event, the three Panhards were crewed by South Africans but the H60 broke down in short order so leaving just two H90s to confront the MPLA/Cuban armoured force advancing on Nova Lisboa with T-34/85 and PT-76 tanks. On 5 October, the SADF/UNITA group moved westwards to meet the enemy. It comprised one Toyota Hilux 'technical' mounting a 14.5mm 'Dushka' heavy machine-gun with a UNITA crew; two UNITA Panhard H90s with SADF crews; one SADF Land Rover ATGW

command vehicle; three SADF ATGW Land Rovers armed with ENTAC ATGW missiles; one SADF Land Rover equipped with twin Browning M2 heavy machine-guns; and, in the rear, two Mercedes Benz cargo trucks loaded with combat supplies. This meagre force was supported by various UNITA infantry elements that were met en route.

Battle was joined overlooking the Caala river near the town of Norton de Matos. In the opening exchange of fire, the command vehicle of Maj Louis 'Holly' Holzhausen was struck and destroyed but fortunately without serious injury to the four-man crew, including the major. He immediately ordered the two Panhards forward to engage the enemy with direct fire. The heavy return bombardment caused the UNITA infantry to flee the battlefield leaving just 18 South Africans to continue the action.

Pinpoint targets such as mortar positions were destroyed by ENTAC missiles while the Panhards under the command of Lt Nel van Rensburg and Cpl F.J.S. Scheepers employed fire and movement to pound the enemy: the former firing 11 HE and four HEAT rounds in the first hour of contact. A flanking attack by some 150 Cuban infantry, discernible by their long hair, was cut down by the machine gun-armed Land Rover. Once this threat was overcome, both sides

BELOW With the failure of the T-34/85 on the battlefield, the Soviet Union soon supplied the far more formidable T-54/55 series in quantity. The F1 90mm gun was hard-pressed to destroy these tanks except at short range and with well-placed rounds. Here a column of vehicles of 32 Battalion pass a knocked-out T-54 during Operation 'Askari' in January 1984, showing the diminutive size of the Eland David against the T-54 Goliath.

withdrew to lick their wounds. Lt van Rensburg in his H90 claimed the destruction of one Soviet armoured vehicle and damage to another. The enemy left some 60 dead on the battlefield while UNITA losses were two soldiers killed and several wounded. The South Africans suffered just one casualty in Sgt K.D. Strauss, the commander of the disabled Panhard, who was slightly injured when the command vehicle was hit. After the battle, Maj Holzhausen withdrew all the SADF assets back to Silva Porto. The enemy assault on Nova Lisboa and the UNITA headquarters was halted for the time being.

Although hardly more than a skirmish, the encounter at Norton de Matos prompted the South African government to become committed, albeit reluctantly, to the War in Angola – a term not used by politicians since the campaign was to remain secret as long as possible, so all military activity in the region was known as 'An dem Bren' or 'Op die Grens' – 'On the Border' – whether it was in Angola or in South West Africa. At the behest of US Secretary of State Henry Kissinger, the government authorised an armed incursion codenamed Operation 'Savannah' into Angola by the SADF employing 'flying columns' in the best Boer 'commando' tradition. The main force was Task Force Zulu with various combat teams joining as reinforcements as the operation gathered momentum, such as Foxbat, Orange and X-Ray. The offensive was launched on 14 October with the aim of blunting the MPLA advance towards the border of South West Africa and relieving the pressure on the FNLA and UNITA before the deadline of 11 November 1975. However, the government imposed strict limitations with just 3,000 South African troops and a maximum of 600 vehicles of all sorts allowed in Angola for the entirety of Operation 'Savannah'. Accordingly, the troops were obliged to requisition civilian vehicles wherever they could with each Task Force having its own retinue of 'vegetable and fruit trucks' as infantry personnel carriers.

The latter is indicative of the paucity of SADF equipment committed to the operation beyond the ubiquitous 'Landie' or Land Rover. As a case in point the commander of Task Force Zulu, Col Koos van Heerden, was provided with a civilian Toyota Land Cruiser as his

TASK FORCE ZULU, OPERATION 'SAVANNAH'

- OC Task Force Zulu – Col Koos van Heerden.
- Battle Group Alpha – Kommandant Delville Linford with three rifle companies of Caprivian and Angolan bushmen.
- Battle Group Bravo – Kommandant Jan Breytenbach with three companies of semi-trained FNLA soldiers.
- Battle Group Charlie – Maj Toon Slabbert with four armoured car troops with support vehicles. A fifth troop was added at Sa da Bandeira.
- No offensive air support was available to Task Force Zulu.
- The only aerial support was transport aircraft for supplies and casualty evacuation. Use was also made of a light aircraft for reconnaissance purposes from time to time, but under strict restricted conditions.
- No SADF military trucks to be used but civilian Land Cruisers, Land Rovers and requisitioned Portuguese trucks.
- No detailed maps were available so tourism maps of Angola were used.
- No SADF uniforms were to be worn but the men were kitted out with former Portuguese weapons, uniforms (also surplus prisoner uniforms) and equipment.
- Only English was to be used for formal communications on the radios.
- Task Force Zulu seldom operated as a single unit. On a day-to-day basis the infantry companies of Task Force Alpha and Bravo were given specific tasks and teamed up with different armoured car troops from Task Force Charlie.

TASK FORCE ZULU – ROUTE, OPERATION 'SAVANNAH'

- Naulila to Rocades – 65km.
- Rocades to Joao de Almeida – 245km.
- Joao de Almeida to Sa da Bandeira – 68km.
- Sa da Bandeira to Cacula – 89km.
- Cacula to Quilengues – 53km.
- Quilengues to Chongoroi – 63km.
- Chongoroi to Catengue – 67km.
- Catengue to Caibambu – 33km.
- Caibambu to Cubal – 29km.
- Cubal to Catengue - 62km.
- Catengue to Benguela – 75km.
- Benguela to BaiaFarta – 44km.
- Benguela to Lobito – 50km
- Lobito to Novo Redondo – 178km.
- Novo Redondo to Alto Hama – 260km.
- Alto Hama to Cela – 112km.

command vehicle. With fewer than 500 men, Task Force Zulu crossed the border at Kalwabi and motored northwards. There were few maps beyond tourist guides and those picked up at Caltex service stations despite the best efforts of 47 Survey Section that had produced reams of official military maps that were misplaced in Grootfontein. In order to keep their presence within Angola a secret, the South Africans went to sometimes excessive lengths. Any item of South African origin was forbidden, down to toothbrushes and bars of soap. The SADF nutria coveralls were withdrawn and troops were supplied with green ones or Portuguese camouflage uniforms; 'takkies' replaced boots and a strange 'staaldak' (steel helmet) was issued. Similarly R1 rifles were taken away and enemy weapons such as AK-47s and PPsH sub machine-guns were provided. Takkies are rubber-soled canvas shoes that are totally unsuited to combat and soon fell apart, so on occasions Eland turret crews had to fight barefoot since the driver had priority in usable footwear. Similarly the green uniforms issued for Operation 'Savannah' were surplus stocks of overalls from the South African prison service, again hardly adequate for use in battle. If captured, SADF troops were told to say that they were mercenaries and in some ways they were as the USA was to pay each soldier Rand (R) 10 a day danger money and South Africa R5; whether such a bounty was actually paid was another matter.

By 19 October, the southern district capital of Pereira d'Eca was captured against little resistance. On the following day, the first Eland armoured cars of D Squadron, 2 Special Service Battalion (SSB), joined Task Force Zulu together with mortar attachments to augment its firepower and speed the advance. More Elands and mortars were attached on 24 October with the capture of the important MPLA town of Sá da Bandeira. The commander of D Squadron, Maj Toon Slabbert, relates the extraordinary measures taken to disguise the presence of SADF troops:

'Every label on the ration tins had to be removed so potentially every meal came as a surprise when my favourite was Vienna Sausages. Fortunately my crew (Troepies Smuts and Kruger) had memorised the NATO Stock Numbers on every tin so no more surprises. I must say I was also partial to Cuban rations, particularly the cheese. To maintain secrecy we were supposed to speak in English over the radio but once combat was joined everyone lapsed into Afrikaans as that was how we were all trained. Even the Bibles we had were in English, which was a problem in my unit as the Padre only knew Afrikaans.

'As so often is the case with AFVs the Eland became more reliable the more you used it. In Angola my Eland travelled some 5,700km without mishap. This was due largely to the "Tiffies" of the Technical Service Corps. In my squadron I was privileged to have two exceptional Tiffy sergeants – Hans Burger and "Kokkie" de Kok. As a case in point one of my Elands broke down with a blown engine so I said to Kokkie "I need this Ninety as soon as possible". So while the march continued with the vehicle under tow he detached the wiring looms, fuel lines, engine bolts etc. He then

ABOVE AND LEFT
Tiffies manhandle an engine change out of an Eland 60 and undertake repairs in the field, thus ensuring the serviceability of AFVs on operations that would soon grind to a halt without their dedication and expertise.

ABOVE An essential adjunct to all armour operations during the Border War was the unceasing support of the 'Tiffies' of the Technical Service Corps who kept the vehicles functional under the most demanding conditions. Here, a Withings 6 x 6 mine-protected recovery vehicle comes to the aid of a disabled Eland 60.

asked me to stop the column for 10min while the tiffies exchanged the engine and then we continued on our way as they reattached all the necessary components. By the time we arrived at our destination the Ninety was up and running. Similarly Hans Burger knew the Eland so intimately that he would stand at the camp gate as the Elands returned from patrol and would indicate as each approached to either park up or go to the tiffies, purely by the sound of the engine and transmission. That is why the Elands were so successful in Angola. We let nothing stop us in action.'

Nicknamed 'Rommel' within the SADF because of his daring and speed of action, Col 'Corky' van Heerden describes the tactics he employed for Task Force Zulu:

'In essence, we proceeded with a small element in front and larger elements to the rear. A troop or two of armoured cars and a platoon of infantry would lead, going as fast as they could. Any likely position would be shot up – simply sowed with bullets. If no one fired back, you carried on. If someone did fire at you, you took cover and then your fight began … .We caught them flat-footed every time. It just goes to show you. They knew we were near by or on the way, but they did not know precisely where we were. We also caught them unprepared by moving as fast as possible when we got going.'

And the advance was at a remarkable rate averaging 90km a day. Task Force Zulu travelled a distance of 3,159km through hostile territory in 33 days on the move, successfully winning every single one of the 51 actions, large and small, it fought, all at a cost of 4 South Africans killed and 20 wounded. It was a triumph by any military standards.

LEFT An Eland 90 and 60 wait their turn at a refuelling point during deployment 'on the border' – the euphemism to denote an operation inside Angola. In the background is a Ratel 20 infantry combat vehicle that was first employed during the Border War in 1976. Thereafter it became the standard AFV of the mechanised infantry battalions. When fitted with the same turret as the Eland 90 it became an anti-tank system in its own right and essentially superseded the role of the Eland.

In many ways the title of Task Force or Battle Group was somewhat of a misnomer since they were synonymous at this time. In such a large country as Angola, the force was often split into subordinate units. A typical column would comprise up to a company of UNITA infantry, keen but inadequately trained, and an SADF element of artillery, armour, engineers, supply, technical services and headquarters personnel. These would have some 50 military vehicles as well as eight G1 25pdr (88mm) or G2 5.5in (140mm) guns of Second World War vintage, and up to, although rarely, a squadron of armoured cars with five troops, each of four Elands both 'Sixty' and 'Ninety', with two more in squadron headquarters. It thus fell to the Eland armoured cars and the artillery to be the offensive arm of any advance into Angola. However, the arms of service had not trained together to any extent previously and much had to be learned in action, as was the case in the Battle of Luso.

The Battle of Luso

After a series of high-level politico-military meetings, the Chief of the Army consequently ordered Commandant A.P.R. Carstens, the Officer Commanding 1 Special Service Battalion (1SSB), to prepare and declare combat ready an entire 22-vehicle Eland armoured car squadron. On 9 October 1975 this squadron, under the command of the 2i/c Capt George Schoeman departed Bloemfontein with 22 Eland armoured cars and 82 crewmen and headed north. Six days and 2,400km later the complete squadron reported battle-ready at Ondangwa in northern South West Africa (SWA), no mean feat considering the vehicles had just been upgraded with new 2.5-litre Ranger engines and that the heat range on the spark plugs had been incorrectly set. Between 17 and 22 October 1975, the entire squadron was air transported to Silva Porto, two vehicles and three 200-litre drums of petrol per flight. The squadron's echelon was completed with the acquisition of five cargo vehicles that had been abandoned by their previous Portuguese owners in the town.

Sgt Johann Olivier was part of Task Force X-Ray and recounts the opening phase of

ABOVE On arrival from France, each AML armoured car came with an equipment schedule of 16 shackles. The SAAC thought this was excessive and decided that five were sufficient for any recovery operation until trials for air transport were conducted. It was then discovered that the 16 were necessary to spread the load of the AML to lashing points inside transport aircraft such as the C-160 Transall and C-130 Hercules. It was by these means that the first Elands were deployed into Angola during Operation 'Savannah'.

Operation 'Savannah' following his deployment from South Africa:

'We were flown to Grootfontein in South West Africa where we received our equipment for the campaign. Due to international sensibilities, our cover was that we were "mercenaries". We were also told that in case of capture we were on our own. We were encouraged to grow beards and look as piratical as possible to further enforce the notion that we were mercenaries and not a regular force. We were then flown by C-130 Flossies to the central Angolan highlands. We drove our fully loaded vehicles right into the rear of the aircraft. After a flight of many hours at treetop level to avoid SAM missiles we landed at a city then known as Silva Porto, which was the UNITA headquarters in Angola. Here we became known as Task Force X-Ray consisting of about 200 men including infantry, two batteries of dated Second World War artillery, three Eland armoured cars, fuel trucks, an ambulance and supply vehicles. We formed a self-contained flying column. We were on our own and would have limited access to further provisions or aid.

'Our objective was to secure central and north-east Angola. Accordingly we struck out

BELOW The armoured bulldozer that became known as the Luso Monster displays the penetration strikes by the 90mm HEAT rounds of the Eland armoured car commanded by Sgt Maj Joe de Vries at the Battle of Luso.

across the endless bush towards the border of Zaire that lies to the north and east of Angola. Our challenges were many: there were barely roads to speak of, very little water, dramatic thunderstorms and flooding, insects, parasites, a variety of dangerous animals as well as diseases like malaria. In addition we were involved in frequent skirmishes with our enemy, the MPLA and the Cubans. Due to our excellent training and preparation, most resistance was fairly easily overcome and we progressed at a good pace until we reached the regional capital Luso – a fairly large city with a modern airport that was vital to both sides.'

There ensued a pitched battle for the airport and town that involved all the various elements of Task Force X-Ray but particularly the artillery and armoured cars fighting in close cooperation. One of the immediate problems was to differentiate between the detonation of a 90mm Eland round and that of the G1 88mm 25pdr gun since this caused some confusion for the artillery observation officers. The first assault on the town failed. In one encounter a large armoured bulldozer was at the head of a counter-attack in the pouring rain. Painted in a garish camouflage scheme it became known as the 'Monster of Luso'. Sgt Johan Olivier was unfortunate to be in its path: 'It had recoilless rifles and machine guns built above the blade, which was welded into a fixed position. It came towards us firing. Our Elands engaged it and we saw at least four shells strike home but the bulldozer just kept on coming though it had stopped firing. We kept up a withering fire but it seemed impervious. Just as it seemed we would have to abandon our position, it ground to a halt. Once we had secured the city and airport, we found that the first couple of rounds from the Elands had killed the crew but missed the motor entirely. The bulldozer then simply continued forward until it got stuck in a ditch.'

The monster was dead and Task Force X-Ray had achieved its aims.

The Battle of Ebo

The Battle of Ebo occurred on Sunday 23 November 1975. It had been preceded by a South African intervention in Angola that had resulted in a lightning advance by its two vanguard Task Forces: Zulu, commanded by Kommandant Jan Breytenbach, and Foxbat, commanded by Kommandant Eddie Webb. Both Task Forces had rendezvoused near the town of Lobito after Zulu had taken it on the 7th, to allow for a brief pause of the offensive in the light of a political reassessment of the situation in Angola. When it became apparent that the Portuguese government would not recognise the MPLA as the sole governing authority of the country on the original deadline of the 11th, both Task Forces were mobilised to resume their offensives towards Luanda, with Zulu pushing up along the coast towards Nova Redondo, and Foxbat making for the inland Santa Comba–Quibala route that ultimately terminated in the Angolan capital.

With the town of Quibala established as their immediate objective, Foxbat pushed north under the new command of Kommandant George Kruys after Kommandant Eddie Webb had been repatriated to South Africa. Their progress on the route north was substantially delayed by a number of skirmishes south of the town of Ebo, by terrain that made travel off-road very difficult and, crucially, by the destruction of a number of bridges over the Nhia river by Cuban and FAPLA sappers. With 'Savannah' at risk of bogging down, the South African-led Task Force had conducted several reconnaissances-in-force around Ebo in the following weeks, looking to push north of the Nhia river beyond it and to get movement towards Quibala restarted. The town of Ebo itself had been inadvertently captured by one such probe on 15 November and when FAPLA responded in force, the reconnaissance team beat a hasty retreat in the face of heavy rocket attacks and a strong ground force. The area was by then beset by bouts of heavy rains, which made large stretches of marshy terrain off the roads impassable by either Eland or vegetable truck-cum-troop-carrier. Probing attacks towards Conde in the west had been warded off by heavy indirect fire pre-registered on the roads, prompting the Task Force to pause and reconsider its options.

Thereafter, Kruys had decided to proceed north again in force, this time with G1 howitzers in indirect fire support and with both of his Combat Teams at full complement. Kruys detached Combat Team Alpha, under Maj Louis Holtzhausen, to flank to the west via Conde. Combat Team Bravo, under Capt Johann Holm, would travel north and attempt to cross the Nhia at Hengo, but upon arrival there they found the bridge destroyed. After seeing off the FAPLA element probing for ambush opportunities, Bravo fell back to Quissobi where they rejoined Combat Team Alpha. Alpha had found the going extremely difficult in hilly terrain and with bad roads and had been re-tasked with the reconstruction of a bridge over the river Tunga that would reopen the road to Ebo. With orders issued to bypass the town and probe north of it for a crossing issued on the 22nd, Combat Team Bravo set off at first light on the 23rd.

Holm's Combat Team consisted of an experienced squadron of 22 Eland armoured cars, under the command of Lt J.C. du Raan and a company each of UNITA and FNLA infantry under the commands of Capts Willie Strydom and Jock Harris respectively. The Combat Team's organic 81mm and 107mm mortar sections had been further supplemented with a troop of Second World War-vintage 25pdrs under the command of Maj P.C. Venter. Overhead, a Cessna 185 flown by Lt Keith Williamson from the South African Air Force's 11 Squadron provided aerial reconnaissance.

Upon reaching Ebo, Combat Team Bravo fired a few probing rounds into the town but received no response despite Williamson's reports that there had been heavy activity some hours earlier. The Combat Team found the town well abandoned after pressing up, its defenders having melted away into the two hills – Dondo and Luanda – to its north. Beyond and to the north-east of Luanda, a peak of some 1,905m, lay the Mabasa river. The road north passed both these features and bridged the Mabasa approximately 5km north of Ebo, and was flanked on its east by thick brush and a coffee plantation. After probing through the town the lead Eland troop commanded by

Lt J.W. Swanepoel and its accompanying FNLA infantry were attacked with an RPG launched from Dondo. Fired at long range it had missed, but it provoked a strong South African response as Swanepoel's troop set off in pursuit. In the meanwhile, the rest of the column followed along in parallel on the road north-east, led by the Eland troop of Lt Johan Du Toit.

Upon reaching the site from which the first RPG attack had been launched, Swanepoel and his troop found the location deserted. However, fresh tyre tracks in the muddy ground and abandoned recovery tools indicated that a vehicle had been stuck, providing evidence that a forward party of FAPLA or Cubans had been present, and Swanepoel opened probing fire into the bush to his north-east. Unlike FAPLA, who either ran or retaliated immediately and thus gave away their positions, the ambushing party remained disciplined and stealthy. Overhead, Williamson could not see much from within his scouting aircraft until a group of fighters emerged near the Mabasa bridge along with a truck. Swanepoel and his troop opened fire on them but as they did not have sight of the bridge, the 30-odd rounds of 90mm they levelled was ineffective despite being provided with a bearing by Williamson. To make matters worse, as Swanepoel pushed to the north-east and established a line of observation on the Panga–Hengo road that turned right off the main route, two of his Elands bogged down in the muddy terrain. To his left, Du Toit and his troop had pushed up aggressively down the road, with the rest of the Combat Team keeping pace behind.

It was at this point that Du Toit entered the killing ground of a well-sited ambush. Laying in wait in the bush to the east of the road were two companies of Cuban-led FAPLA troops, well equipped with RPG-7s and two SPG-9 recoilless rifles of 73mm calibre. On the other side of the river waited four single-shot Grad-P 122mm rocket launchers, a battery of mortars and artillery that may have included a BM-21 MRLS, and one ZiS-3 76mm field gun employed in the same direct-fire, anti-tank role that had caused serious casualties among German panzers in the Second World War. Manned by a Cuban crew, it was perfectly situated in ambush and registered on target.

Williamson, who had spotted the hostile positions at the last, shouted a warning just as the ambush was sprung.

The 76mm gun's first shot down the road smashed through the thin driver's hatch of Du Toit's Eland and killed Tpr Niel Lombard instantly. Swerving out of control, the Eland skewed off the road and plummeted into the Mabasa river, with Du Toit and his gunner, Cpl J.W. Van der Merwe, still trapped inside. Heavy small-arms fire washed over the following vehicles in the column, punctuated by recoilless rifle and RPG fire. One HEAT round knocked out the third vehicle of the column, that of Cpl Botha, trapping the Eland of Staff Sgt van Ellewee ahead of him. Van der Linden was subsequently shot out and when his vehicle filled with smoke he ordered his crew to bail out. As they did, they returned fire on the ambushers and sought cover in a ditch to their left. Botha decided to play dead instead, with his vehicle particularly exposed as indirect fire exploded around them on pre-registered firing coordinates. The FNLA company that had pushed forward with the Eland were scattered and badly savaged by the ambush, losing some 27 men killed in place. Pulled back under fire by Capt Jock Harris and Cpl Andre Diedericks, the withdrawal would cost them a further 7 killed.

In response, the Combat Team immediately began to retaliate with mortar fires directed by Staff Sgts Steenkamp and Benson in an attempt to suppress the ambushers. This retaliation was cut short by a heavy barrage of accurate 122mm fire that savaged the Bravo mortar position. Benson and 7 of the UNITA mortarists were killed instantly, with Steenkamp and 14 others seriously injured. To the right of the road, Swanepoel pushed up in an attempt to relieve pressure, too, with the Eland of Cpl J.J. Taljaard in support. Taljaard's Eland, however, was bracketed by 122mm fire and then struck in its turret. As it filled with smoke, Taljaard's driver, Tpr G. Volgraaf, bailed from the vehicle and began to run for Ebo before being shot through the stomach by an enemy marksman. With Taljaard and his gunner abandoning their vehicle to carry Volgraaf to the casualty collection station, and his own supply of ammunition shot out, Swanepoel's counter-attack stalled when he too bogged down in the mud. Combat Team Bravo's G1s opened up counter-battery fire from an airstrip just to the north of Ebo, but overshot the forward positions of their enemy and failed to reduce the volume of incoming fire.

On the road, in the meanwhile, some Elands had pressed forward in an attempt to rescue van der Linden, Botha and their crews. The Eland of 2/Lt A.J. 'Bok' Kriel got close, levelling machine-gun fire and HE into the ambusher's trenches, but was struck in its muzzle brake and forced to retire. The next to attempt was Cpl John Wahl, whose vehicle got further and managed to rescue one of Botha's crewmembers, but progressing further became impossible with the squadron's 90mm ammunition all but spent. By now, Capt Holm had arrived on the scene personally, along with a column of reinforcement Elands under the command of Capt Anton Fourie that had been held in reserve. With Bravo's mortars reorganised under WO Jeff Burger and now delivering somewhat effective counter-fire, Fourie's Eland squadron pushed forward and, although inexperienced, it managed to turn the tide.

With the rest of the squadron supressing the ambusher's trenches, the leading Eland commanded by 2/Lt Jan Alberts advanced until it was engaged by the ZiS-3 anti-tank gun. With forewarning of its suspected location, the muzzle blast of the ZiS-3 gave Alberts' gunner a precise target to engage and, after a few close hits with HE, its Cuban crew scattered into the bush. Alberts was then able to advance forward and recover Botha and his crewman, and to then tow out two of the disabled Elands.

Just as the battle had shown signs of stabilising for Combat Team Bravo, however, another disaster struck in the rear. The area around the mortar position had become a collection point for crews that had dismounted from damaged Elands or from those that had withdrawn after expending their ammunition, as well as the wounded. After transferring Tpr Volgraaf to Lt Herman van Niekerk, Cpl J.J. Taljaard had begun assisting the mortar teams, as had 2/Lt A.J. Kriel. Van Niekerk, in turn, had repeatedly shuttled between Ebo and the front with wounded carried in Capt Holm's salvaged blue Honda 4 x 4. Returning after dropping off the mortally wounded Volgraaf with the medics in Ebo, van Niekerk noted WO Burger and his

two troopers hastily evacuating their mortar position. Jumping out to assist, he was joined by Taljaard and Kriel, and together the five men began to load mortar tubes into the waiting trucks of the mortar section just as accurate indirect fire began to bracket their position. Just then, Capt Holm came to a halt next to them, having swapped out his Honda for an Eland 90. Leaning out of the turret to warn the motorists that they had been ranged, Holm was exposed when a salvo of 122mm rockets hit. Holm and Taljaard were both killed instantly, while Lts Kriel and van Niekerk were wounded. Both lieutenants would ultimately drive themselves out of the battle, despite their wounds.

Capt Fourie, in the meanwhile, was tasked with recovering the lost Eland and covering the withdrawal. Botha's disabled Eland was towed back to the collection point and two of Swanepoel's stuck vehicles were also recovered. Swanepoel's two forwardmost Elands, however, could not be retrieved while stuck in the mud up to their axles and while under fire, and were destroyed in place to prevent capture. Due to a miscommunication confusing these with the Eland of Lt du Toit and L/Cpl Ellewee, Capt Fourie believed his mission accomplished and began to withdraw south under the orders of Kommandant Kruys. Du Toit and his gunner, Cpl van der Merwe, would wait until nightfall in the flooding remains of their Eland, with enemy patrols passing within 50m of them at times. They, along with Ellewee

and his crew, would successfully escape back south, with their vehicles eventually recovered by the MPLA and displayed in Ebo as monuments to the battle.

In all, South African casualties at Ebo amounted to 8 killed, 5 mortally wounded on the 23rd, and 3 on the following day when Lt Williamson's Cessna was shot down in the area on a reconnaissance mission. FNLA/UNITA losses amounted to at least 41 deaths, with numbers of wounded numbering into the 80s. While demoralising and humbling to an extent, the battle was not, however, a signal defeat of Task Force Foxbat. Despite the loss of four Elands, Foxbat remained an effective combat force that could muster two squadrons of Eland armoured cars at nearly full strength. Reinforced with a battery of G2 140mm guns and given time to reorganise and repair, Foxbat would redeploy offensively that December, crossing the Nhia river in the face of fierce enemy resistance at one of the few crossing points that had not been completely destroyed by the enemy.

The Battle of Bridge 14

Known prosaically as Bridge 14, it was to become one of the most significant encounters of Operation 'Savannah'. The historian of Rhodesian and South African military affairs, Richard Allport, gives a graphic account of the battle that started on 4 December:

'Troops were sent to nearby high ground named Top Hat and Hippo Hill where they set up Artillery Observation Posts from which they could see the bridge. They were also able to observe the enemy setting up mortar positions in a nearby kraal and called in South African artillery fire, which soon eliminated the position. The observers were also able to direct fire onto an armoured car and against a rooi oog (red eye) rocket position, both of which were destroyed. Later, from this vantage point, the South Africans were able to watch Angolan and Cuban troops wading in the river near the site of the bridge. Again they called in artillery fire, creating havoc among the surprised enemy, the continuously exploding shells killing many of them. Reinforcements arrived for the Cuban/FAPLA force in the first week of December and

set up an HQ and ammunition dump just north of the river.'

(The rooi oog or 'red eye' was the SADF nickname for the 122mm rocket that had a range of 19km and a flight time of 12sec as it trailed bright red flames and smoke indicating its direction of travel. This usually gave troops sufficient time to seek shelter.)

'By 9 December the enemy had withdrawn to positions further back from the river and had abandoned attempts to hold the bridge, mainly because of the devastatingly accurate South African artillery fire. The rest of the troops of the South African combat group were brought forward to take up positions near the south side of the bridge. The sappers sweated to get the bridge ready in time and at first light on 12 December the South African artillery prepared for a supreme effort. The morning was misty and the artillery was delayed in starting its bombardment until the enemy targets became visible to the observers.'

One of the artillery observers on Hippo Hill was Lt Johan Potgieter, a battery commander of 1 Medium Battery, 4 Field Regiment. He was directing the 5.5in or 'Vyf Vyf' guns emplaced on the southern side of the Nhia river. Below him lay the MPLA/Cuban defence lines including some captured UNITA Sabre Land Rovers (supplied by the CIA) and a BRDM armoured car (supplied by the Soviet Union) covering Bridge 14.

'I ordered a troop fire mission, applied a "drop 200" correction, ordered five rounds fire for effect, airburst at my command and waited for the right moment. The MAPLA troops were totally unaware when I ordered fire and some 50sec later all hell broke loose. Black smoke puffs and the bright detonations of the proximity fuses covered the whole target. The troops at the Sabres were sliced down. I gave an "add 50" correction and ordered 20 rounds [of] fire for effect. One of the Ladas (staff car) started burning. The driver in the BRDM panicked. He tried to reverse, but skidded around like a Jack Russell playing with a rag. Somehow, the cable snapped and the BRDM started to move out onto the road. I ordered a fire mission on number one gun, as "Gas" Liebenberg's gun crew were the fastest and most accurate, and applied a small correction to intercept the vehicle on the road some 200m ahead. The gun reacted remarkably quickly, considering the range of approximately 9,000m. The first round landed just in front of the vehicle, forcing it to stop. The next round fell slightly short, but thanks to the driver's hesitation, the third round landed right on top of the BRDM. The detonation wave virtually lifted the rear of the vehicle up and plunged it into a sand embankment. We only found out later that the officer in the Lada was Commandante Raúl Diaz Argüelles, the overall commander of the internationalist operation in Angola, a hero of the anti-Batista struggle and an extremely popular figure in Cuba, who died on the spot.'

Cuban accounts differ and suggest Argüelles was killed in a BRDM that struck a mine together with two Cuban senior Special Forces officers – perhaps it is more seemly to die for your country in an armoured fighting vehicle than a Lada. Nevertheless it was a significant blow to the communist campaign in Angola. Counter-battery fire from BM21 multiple rocket launchers now rained down on the South African positions and the engineers rebuilding Bridge 14. As Allport recounts, the attack by the infantrymen and armoured cars was scheduled to take place in three phases: first, a central attack by Eland armoured cars and a company of infantry to drive the enemy back towards Bridge 15 near Cassamba; second, an attack by a company of infantry to take the kraal; and finally, an attack by a company of infantry on the hill positions to capture the high ground and then link up with the armoured cars of phase one:

'Ranged against them was over 1,000 infantry, many of them Cuban troops. Further back were anti-tank weapons, including Sagger missiles, deployed to cover the road that Foxbat would have to advance along. In their second defence line FAPLA had several 120mm Cuban-manned mortars, 76mm guns, and an entire battery of 14.7mm anti-aircraft guns together with 122mm multiple rocket launchers. Most of the enemy positions had been carefully pinpointed during the preceding days by forward observers and recce troops and when the South Africans started with the heaviest artillery barrage of the battle, the enemy was taken by surprise. Some of FAPLA's ammunition

trucks were hit and exploded. Enemy artillery positions were hit and wiped out, the Cuban mortars receiving direct hits, killing most of the crews, and within a few hours the South African artillery commanded the battlefield.'

From his vantage point on Hippo Hill, Potgieter observed:

'The air was filled with an orange mushroom cloud followed by the loudest explosion I have ever heard. The barrage rolled onto the second defensive position consisting of 76mm field guns, anti-aircraft guns and 120mm mortars, and suddenly the enemy cracked. The few remaining vehicles started moving towards the tarred road leading through Catofe to Quibala. After a few minutes, at least 50 vehicles of all sorts were on the road trying their best to overtake the one in front. I ordered two guns to fire continuous fire – in other words until I told them to stop – on a point about 1,000m ahead of these vehicles where a rocky outcrop covered in thick bush stretched across the tarred road. The embankments on either side of the road were very steep and all vehicles had to pass through this point. The front five vehicles drove into the fire and were destroyed. I ordered the other two guns onto single fire missions on the same road and gradually bunched the whole convoy in by firing at the rear of the convoy. As the fall of shot was adjusted, more and more vehicles were destroyed; eventually 12 wrecked vehicles were connected like a train. The enemy soldiers jumped out and scrambled into the bush and some of them started running towards the point where the other two guns were firing at. I stopped the engagement. They were neutralised anyway and we could do with a few vehicles.'

The first troop of armoured cars rolled over the bridge and fanned out to either side of the road so avoiding the killing zone of Sagger ATGW and 76mm guns. Firing continuously, the Elands advanced about 500yd forcing enemy infantry to retreat. One of the armoured cars surprised a mortar position, destroying six mortars with one of its 90mm shells. When they ran out of ammunition a further three Elands were sent in to take their place. In command of the second troop was Lt Lou 'Vannie' van Vuuren, and he takes up the story:

'We had deployed about five klicks into the bush past the bridge (Bridge 14) when I got a radio message asking if I knew of any friendly infantry approaching from my rear. I didn't know of any. In fact I was sure there were none so I figured it must be Cubans. We had encountered them before. They fight a little better than the Angolans, but not much. They're always high on dagga (marijuana). Nearly all the dead we examined and the prisoners we captured had dagga on them. At any rate my troop of three Elands had relieved a troop of five. We were told that there was some enemy, including tanks, approaching. I moved the troop to the top of a hill where we had a good field of fire. We were soon engaged by the enemy and my co-axial machine gun and roof-mounted Browning were knocked out leaving me with just the 90mm main armament. That firing died down so we returned to the tarred road when I saw a Russian truck coming up from behind. At first we thought it was one we had captured earlier but it wasn't. It was loaded with about 30 Cubans.

'At first I observed them through the periscope and then when the truck came alongside I opened the hatch for a closer look. The Cubans were laughing and one was playing a guitar. One of them gave me the V peace sign with his fingers as they went by, which I returned. I let them get about 10m ahead and then let one loose from the 90. Truck and Cubans sort of disappeared. We carried on. I posted two cars in good fire support positions and went ahead on recce. I soon came across a kuka (bush store) with a Land Rover carrying two fuel drums parked outside as well as a group of Cubans. They were all standing around in the rain waving their hands in the air and arguing. There seemed to be no leadership so I suppose they were all high on dagga. We fired another 90 into them and they virtually disintegrated. We heard then of more infantry coming up the road. I decided we couldn't capture the Land Rover so I fired my last round into it.

'As we were trying to rejoin the other two Elands my engine died. Soon the Cubans were climbing all over the vehicle so there we were with both machine guns knocked out and no ammunition for the 90. My driver, Tommy Corns, then reminded me about my sidearm

(Star 9mm semi-automatic pistol). I pulled it out of the holster and shifted it to my left hand since I had injured my right hand during the firefight. I started shooting out of a firing slit and got four of them with the first magazine. I reloaded and in the excitement forgot about my sore right hand so fired with it and got seven more Cubans. By this time there seemed to be only one of them left. He was lying down near the side of the road firing at us with an AK-47. Fortunately for us none of the Cubans had any RPGs with them. Tommy wanted to run right over him but that didn't seem fair to me and I thought maybe we could just scare him off so we headed for him. Unfortunately he didn't move so we drove straight over him and another Cuban behind him we hadn't noticed. By now all the tyres had been shot up so we were moving on run-flats (the Eland can travel some 50km on run-flat tyres). By now all the Cubans were either dead or had fled.'

The armoured cars had advanced so rapidly that the infantry had been unable to keep up with them. Phase two of the attack had been carried out according to plan, with little resistance being offered at the kraal, which had been abandoned by the enemy after the South African artillery shells began to land on it. They left their heavy weapons and ammunition behind. By 12.00hrs the attack had been completed and the troops began to consolidate their positions. An hour later it had begun to rain heavily and troop movement was severely hindered, although the engineers continued to work on the bridge. The road to Quibala was now open but to no avail.

The action had lasted some six hours and over 400 of the enemy were killed at a cost of 4 South African dead. It was a prime example of the superior training and motivation of South African troops and Eland crews in particular, admirably supported by the artillery and engineers. For his gallantry Lt van Vuuren was awarded the Honoris Crux or Cross of Honour, equivalent to Distinguished Service Cross in the American military or the Military Cross in the British. For the rest of his military career in which he rose to the rank of brigadier general, Lou van Vuuren was commonly known as 'Pistol Port' from his expertise with his Star sidearm. Three other Honoris Crux

were awarded for heroism during the Battle of Bridge 14.

During Operation 'Savannah', five squadrons of Elands were deployed to Angola numbering over 100 armoured cars. The major problem was finding the manpower to crew them in combat. This was exemplified by the experiences of candidate officer Chris Gildenhuys:

'I was called up in January 1975 to serve with 1SSB at Bloemfontein. On the first day I was selected to do leadership training at the School of Armour. The largest group of conscripts was to be taught on the Eland with two smaller classes on tanks and support troops acting as armoured infantry, although they were still equipped with Bedford RL trucks. As I had a driving licence, I started on the Driving and Maintenance Course for Elands. Like several others I was too tall to fit in the Eland when driving so I had to sit on the battery box with no backrest to be able to engage the foot pedals. Furthermore, in that position it was impossible to see through the vision blocks of the driver's hatch so we drove with the hatch open all the time – not necessarily sensible in combat. The problem was largely overcome with the introduction of the Eland Mk 6 that had a longer and larger hull. Training on the 60 and

90mm weapons followed before I was chosen together with four other candidate officers to go to C Squadron 2SSB at Zeerust on 28 November 1975.

'It was an enormous learning curve to be a troop commander of 4 Elands and 11 men, mostly inexperienced conscripts, as well as a huge responsibility. On 8 December, we were flown by Flossie (C-130 Hercules) to Grootfontein where we acquired our Elands and logistic vehicles from 16 Maintenance Unit to form a battle group of one armoured car squadron, one artillery battery of G2 140mm (5.5in) howitzers and an HQ element under the command [of] Kommandant Yvor de Bruyn. The Eland squadron was led by the legendary Maj Fido Smit and WO1 Ben van Balen as Squadron Sergeant Major. The latter immediately became our father figure and took complete control through wise counsel and guidance to us inexperienced junior officer troops. Late in the afternoon, we travelled north to Angola where we crossed the border at Oshikango. Driving on dirt roads was extremely tiring so the crews took it in turns until we arrived at our laager position on the golf course at Lobito on the west coast of the country.

'From there we conducted daily patrols along

ABOVE Throughout Operation 'Savannah' there was a woeful lack of combat engineers to expedite the advance of all the disparate battle groups. This became all the more serious in the latter stages as the enemy conducted a concerted delaying action by demolishing all bridges to impede the progress of South African units. Because of its low weight of just 5 tonnes, the Eland is relatively simple to transport across rivers and waterways on engineer pontoons as shown here during an exercise.

ABOVE AND BELOW An Eland crew of 1 Light Horse Regiment display the tools of their trade of 90mm HE and practice rounds, as well as 250-round belts of 7.62mm Browning machine-gun ammunition, while the two kneeling troepies hold bottles of Old Brown Sherry – that essential item taken on exercises and operations that (by pure coincidence) fit snugly into the 81mm smoke grenade launchers. *(William Surman)*

the coast to observe any ships approaching Angola; guarded bridges; and kept the roads protected for supply vehicles for the troops operating further north to whom we acted as a reserve. On 19 December, Fido Smit reminded us that a passing out parade was being held at the School of Armour for our intake so he decided we would have our own ceremony under a big thorn tree on the golf course. It was conducted by Lt André Venter (having returned to duty following a gunshot wound) who cut out cardboard stars with scissors and glued them as 2nd lieutenant pips on the shoulders of our coveralls. We were then given a cup of toxic Portuguese brandy to celebrate the event although my good friend Herbie Welman looked decidedly sick with suspected malaria and immediately took to his bed. Nevertheless he woke up the next day as fit as a fiddle so the foul liquor must have cured him of his ills. In the ten weeks I was on Operation "Savannah", my troop never fired a shot in anger before we withdrew in February 1976.'

On 9 February 1976, the US Congress ratified the Clark Amendment whereupon the West's tacit support for South Africa's intervention in Angola evaporated together with the supply of weapons to UNITA. Deep inside hostile territory, the SADF forces were now a hostage to fortune. Resupply and reinforcement was largely dependent on the South African Air Force flying endless shuttle missions over thousands of miles to deliver on average 1,000 tons of freight and 1,000 passengers per month – virtually the same as achieved by Western air forces during the Berlin Airlift of 1948 but then with a distance of just 200 miles. At one stage the width of the front lines in Angola was 750 miles, which equates to just one Eland armoured car every 7 miles. During Operation 'Savannah', South African casualties amounted to 35 killed in combat and another 10 in accidents. Angolan casualties were numbered in their thousands.

To cover the withdrawal, several Citizen Force reserve units were mobilised including eight infantry regiments, three artillery regiments, numerous support troops and five Eland armoured car regiments including Regiment Oranjerivier, Regiment Mooirivier, Regiment Vrystaat and 1 and 2 Light Horse Regiments as well as C Squadron of the Natal Mounted Rifles equipped with Centurion and Skokiaan tanks. The withdrawal was completed on 27 March 1976. The SADF had achieved its military objectives of preventing any Angola faction from encroaching into South West Africa (Namibia), but the political failure to install a friendly government in Luanda doomed Angola to a further 15 years of bitter warfare. Yet the Eland had proved to be a decisive asset throughout the campaign beyond all expectations. In the words of Kommandant Jay Breytenbach:

'In my mind's eye I can still see them at Catengue, their 90mm guns cracking away at FAPLA in a cauldron of smoke, flames, and fury; and at Benguela in little knots on the airfield under rocket, anti-tank and mortar fire. Wherever they were, they were invariably shooting and manoeuvring towards the enemy, leading the advance with my infantry, deploying at lightning speed and returning fire the moment we hit an enemy position. I remember the bearded, laughing faces of the troop leaders when we sat down to a hasty meal of bread, cheese and beer in Sa da Bandeira. I remember that Toon's Squadron never left my infantry in the lurch. They were always up front with them and supporting them in style whenever and wherever they were required. They were committed to my platoons and they believed my troops were the most professional in Angola. For their part, my troops just loved the armoured cars – especially the devastating bang of the 90mm main gun.'

During Operation 'Savannah' the Noddy Car was triumphant.

The scourge of mines

The greatest threat to vehicles throughout the war was the landmine, invariably of Soviet origin, such as the TM-46 that contained

BELOW From early in its career the diminutive Eland was known as the Noddy Car. To the infantry this was a derisory nickname from the character in children's stories by Enid Blyton, but to the armour fraternity 'Noddy' referred to the vehicle's propensity to rock back on its suspension, as if nodding, on firing the powerful 90mm main armament. So the term Noddy Car became a badge of honour.

Kriel. Both sustained minor wounds, van Zyl a broken nose and Kriel a broken ankle. However, the driver, Tpr D.B. 'David' le Roux, was killed instantly, his body having been thrown backwards into the upright car. The resulting fire completely gutted the vehicle. It was some six hours before the charred and mangled body of the driver could be recovered. Mines were to remain the greatest threat to AFVs throughout the war in Angola and they were particularly damaging to the Eland.

3 Troop, D Squadron, Task Force Zulu

The lack of resources and pusillanimous political direction from Pretoria compromised military operations throughout Operation 'Savannah'. It is fair to say that success on the battlefield time after time was due to the superior training and tenacity of the young South African conscripts in combat. On the principle of 'e pluribus unum', this account relates the exploits of 3 Troop of D Squadron of 2SSB under the command of Lt Andre Venter. 3 Troop along with three other armoured car troops formed part of Battle Group Charlie within Task Force Zulu. The other troops were 1 and 5 Troops of D Squadron under the command of Lt Lusse and Cpl Sakkie Bredenkamp respectively, and later on a 2SSB troop under the command of Lt Nicolaou that became 2 Troop. Their armoured cars were dark green unlike the light desert sand beige of the D Squadron ones. At a later stage, another troop under the command of Lt Nel van Rensburg joined Task Force Zulu at Sa da Bandeira as 4 Troop, also with green cars. The latter were then painted with yellow stripes to suit the Angolan terrain and for mutual recognition. The complete squadron was commanded by Maj Toon Slabbert who, in the words of Kommandant Jan Breytenbach: 'Toon was a giant of a man with flaming red hair and beard. He was a rough diamond and an excellent fighting soldier. He was the only man I had ever seen putting on an Eland armoured car like a pair of underpants, instead of getting into it as other people do. He used the 60 as a command vehicle because his size made it impossible for

ABOVE On 10 October 1975 an Eland was destroyed by a mine containing more than 12kg of explosives. Miraculously, two of the three-man crew survived with minor injuries.

5.7kg of explosives, sufficient to disable the heaviest of AFVs. But on 10 October 1975 an Eland was destroyed by more than 12kg of explosives. The detonation blew the front end of the car straight up into the air, with the vehicle coming to a rest on its rear end. The front wheels were thrown approximately 50m away, while the turret was torn off and deposited behind the car complete with its two occupants, Tprs J.J. 'Koos' van Zyl and L.L.R. 'Lourens' him to ride in a 90 where space was taken up by the big 90mm gun.'

For 3 Troop of D Squadron, Operation 'Savannah' began with disaster. On 12 August, D Squadron deployed from Walvis Bay to Ruacana on the Angolan border, a journey of some 1,000km that took 24hrs before arriving at Ruacana airport. There the crews serviced their weapons when a burst of machine-gun fire shattered the early evening silence. Standing in the turret of his Eland 60, call sign Four Three Charlie, Cpl 'Pottie' Potgieter was struck several times and mortally wounded. Lt André Venter jumped on to the vehicle and tried to lift him from the turret when another single shot rang out hitting Lt Venter in the buttocks, the final round in the Browning having 'cooked off'. To aid a rapid evacuation, the Elands lined the unlit runway to provide illumination with their headlights for an emergency flight to Ondangwa. The next morning 3 Troop was deployed to the Ruacana Border Post that was to become home for the next two months. At this time, 3 Troop comprised four Eland Mk 5

ABOVE Prior to Operation 'Savannah', D Squadron of 2 Special Service Battalion (2SSB) was based at Rooikop at Walvis Bay as armour support to 2 South African Infantry Battalion Group. The topography around Walvis Bay is predominantly sand dunes and scrubland and so the Eland armoured cars were painted accordingly, with this troop of Elands pictured operating in typical terrain. *(Sam van den Berg)*

LEFT D Squadron of 2SSB was commanded by Maj Toon Slabbert and the unit comprised four troops each of four Elands. Each troop comprised two Eland 90s and two Eland 60s (as here) with the Eland 90s at the front and rear of the patrol. The grouping of the 90mm gun in the direct fire mode and the 60mm in the indirect fire mode provided a formidable combination of firepower throughout the Eland's deployment in the Border War.*(Sam van den Berg)*

LEFT The commander of 3 Troop D Squadron was Lt André Venter, seen here looking back at his troop during an exercise in the field. In deep or loose sand the Eland required constant gear shifting to maintain momentum, so it became tiring to drive after a time and once in bush terrain the frequent changes of direction to avoid trees and obstacles led to disorientation on occasions. *(Sam van den Berg)*

LEFT Christened 'CHARMAINE', Eland Mk 5 R11634 was call sign Tango Four Three Charlie, with 'Tango' denoting the Armoured Corps (as in 'Tank'), while 'Four' signifies D Squadron; 'Three' is the troop number and 'Charlie' the third vehicle within the troop. The troop commander's call sign was Four Three Zero; the troop sergeant Four Three Alpha and the other two junior call signs Charlie and Delta. Commonly the troop leader and troop sergeant commanded the AML 90s. *(Sam van den Berg)*

armoured cars with two 'Nineties' and two 'Sixties', the two 90s commanded by Lt Hennie Kotze, as replacement for Lt Venter, and Four Three Alpha by the Trp Sgt, Jan 'Tenk' Fourie, while Bravo and Charlie were the two 60s.

On 14 October, the squadron congregated at Ruacana airport where the Elands were stripped of all insignia including their 'R' registration numbers and camouflaged with green stripes. The troops were issued with green uniforms (it later transpired that they were surplus prison uniforms). On the following evening the squadron entered Angola for the first time – Operation 'Savannah' was under way. The driver of Four Three Charlie, Tpr Sam van den Berg, takes up the story:

LEFT Once deployed to Ruacana on the border with Angola, the yellow Elands of D Squadron 2SSB were camouflaged with green stripes to suit the vegetation, while conversely the green Elands of 1SSB once deployed from South Africa were given brown ochre stripes over their base colour. All unit signs and registration numbers of the Elands were obliterated before the outset of Operation 'Savannah'. *(Sam van den Berg)*

'We were excited to get going after the two-day wait at Calueque. Our first contact came on 20 October 1975 at Rocades, now called Xangongo. We arrived at Rocades early afternoon and from my perspective the battle was remote with mortars and some machine-gun action – really an anti-climax. I remember seeing a "smoke ring" left by an RPG 7. When we arrived at the Fort itself, all was over. I remember a hole in a building left by a 90mm HEAT projectile that went in the one side and out the other without exploding.'

As the firing died down, 3 Troop as well as the rest of the Task Force was involved in mopping up operations around Rocades. It became immediately obvious that FAPLA soldiers, when in trouble, divested themselves of their uniforms and weapons to mingle among the civilian population. Among the abandoned stores were bales of FAPLA uniforms, so

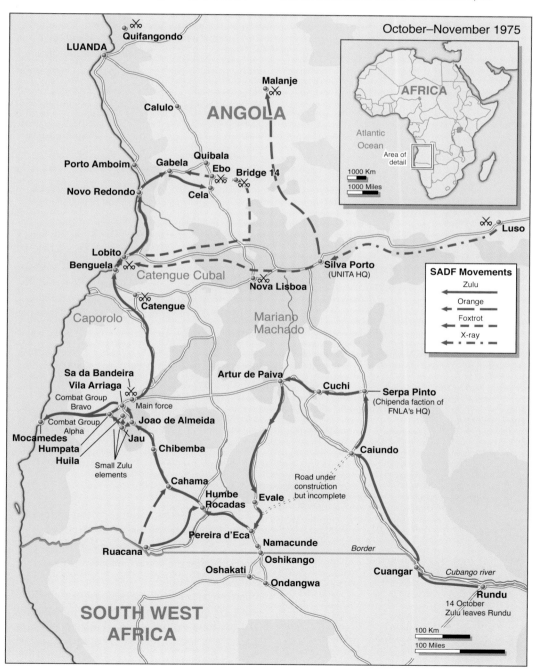

LEFT Task Force Zulu and Operation 'Savannah', October–November 1975.
(Ian Moores)

many of the armoured car crews swapped their 'prison uniforms' for the more fetching camouflage ones. Similarly, the Cuban rations were deemed to be superior, with preferred items including toothpaste-like tubes of condensed milk, tins with tuna and ham, and dry rations such as rice and cornflour as well as Cuban cigarettes and cigars.

The next important objective was the town of Sa da Bandeira with its airport as an important supply point. On the way three ambushes were encountered but quickly overcome. Each site had recoilless guns and a 122mm Red Eye launcher with usually five rockets. Several FAPLA vehicles were shot out. The 82mm recoilless guns presented a real threat to the Elands but fortunately their crews never properly used them until the Battle of Ebo. The attack on Sa da Bandeira Airport began at 15.00hrs on 23 October with the Eland 90s lined up on the main road from where they opened fire. Each 90 fired several shots into the main building without any response from FAPLA. With this bombardment in progress a transport plane carrying FAPLA reinforcements approached the airport but suddenly banked and flew off. The Elands then moved on to the airfield and swept the area for FAPLA soldiers that were dug in at various places on the perimeter. 3 Troop, in conjunction with the Battle Group Bravo infantry and Land Rovers/Cruisers with mounted Brownings and Vickers, drove line-abreast and directed speculative machine-gun fire at all possible FAPLA positions on the airfield. As the

Elands emerged from the built-up area, trucks were seen streaming from a military base on the other side of a river. Even though the distance was beyond the direct fire operational range of the Eland 90s, they were positioned with their rear wheels in a ditch to obtain extra elevation and opened fire artillery-style on the rapidly withdrawing enemy.

By now the speed of the advance accelerated along with the confidence of the SADF troops. In the words of Kommandant Jay Breytenbach: 'We in Task Force Zulu had learned early to remain fully mobile. All we had to do was climb in our vehicles, start them up and head in whatever direction our superiors decreed.' And the next target was Moçamedes, a coastal desert town that was approached by the spectacular Serra da Leba pass. Cpl Ben le Roux, the troop sergeant of 5 Troop, recalls the advance on Mocamedes:

'The area near Moçamedes was semi-desert with only thorn trees and greenery along the dry river courses. On high ground, we several times encountered abandoned ambush locations with vehicles fitted with recoilless cannons and boxes of ammunition next to them. These were obviously meant for us but the enemy was nowhere to be seen. Accordingly anything approaching from the front was considered enemy. Resistance was slight. Along the way a Corolla was destroyed when it was shot out with the co-axial Browning. Hand grenades and other ammunition in the vehicle exploded resulting in Sgt Maj Rohrbeck commenting that we might as well save the 90mm ammunition and just use the Brownings. Few targets justified the 90mm main weapon. We were driving with closed hatches and the road twisted and turned with several hills, resulting in me losing direction.

LEFT The view from the driver's compartment of Tango Four Three Charlie as the Elands of 3 Troop drive through the streets of Sa da Bandeira after the fierce battle for the airport. More than 80 FAPLA soldiers were killed and 30 captured before it was secured on 23 October 1975. On the following day, D Squadron attacked a major FAPLA base or Quartel, forcing the enemy into headlong retreat that became a characteristic of the campaign. *(Sam van den Berg)*

'Suddenly at about 1,500m I noticed a large group of infantry heading for a grass hut. In Task Force Zulu everybody wore uniforms collected along the way. The same applied to FAPLA therefore it was very difficult to distinguish between them and us. Contrary to the norm, where we would simply open fire, I reported the group to Kommandant Linford. He responded "Put one of your HE jobs in there", meaning a 90mm round. We went through the drill and I said "Fire" with my gunner responding "Fire now!" There was only a click. My gunner responded "Sorry corporal, the electrical switch was off." The same drill followed. "Fire!", "Fire now!" Another click. "Sorry corporal the safety clip was on." I looked at him sternly. Suddenly we heard Kommandant Linford over the radio: "Stop, stop, it is the Fletchas, don't shoot, it is the Fletchas." There was almost a disaster. With all the action we did not realise that the road turned 180 degrees and that we are seeing our own Fletchas sweeping the area. Usually they waited until all the dust settled. The good Lord spared them that day and I thank him for it. All our lives would have changed irrevocably had the 90mm gun fired.'

The Portuguese for 'Arrows', the Fletchas were former Portuguese Special Forces troops and the inspiration for the Rhodesian Selous Scouts and the South African Koevoet.

There followed the decisive battle of Catengue on 2 and 3 November that Col van Heerden subsequently stated: 'It was where Task Force Zulu's war was won.' It proved to be the first armed encounter between the SADF and Cuban forces in a war that was to last another 15 years. By now, FAPLA morale was plummeting as Jan Breytenbach declared: 'Our Zulu Force reputation for surprisingly fast movement and unexpected violent action had preceded us. I think many a FAPLA commander had his work cut out to keep his men in position when word got out that we were on the way. It was now the turn of the Cubans.'

As 3 Troop moved north, the gunner of Tango Four Three Zero, Tpr Fred Gericke, shot up a FAPLA Land Rover approaching from Nova Lisboa. By now the Standard Operating Procedure was for the troops to advance by leapfrogging each other in bounds. In Four Three Charlie, Sam van den Berg recalled as 4 Troop passed him on the next bound:

'I joined Phillip and Harry on the turret. At this stage we felt like real veterans and used opportunities such as this to make a cup of coffee or eat something. Suddenly we heard explosions as well as a projectile (Katyusha rocket) going overhead. We also saw smoke around the 4 Troop cars further up the road and realised that they had driven into an ambush. 4 Troop instantly returned fire and soon requested permission to move back to re-arm since they were running out of ammunition. Obviously we also abandoned our tea break and took position inside the car. It was the Charlie car's turn to drive in front so we were quite apprehensive as we moved forward into the killing zone.

'On the way forward we saw some of our infantry wide-eyed and without their rifles running back towards Catengue. The heavy bombardment coupled to the sight of the 4 Troop cars withdrawing had unnerved them and their commanders had considerable trouble in convincing them to go back. We used the (60mm) mortars as well as the machine gun to fire at targets. The inside of the car was filled with smoke and empty 7.62mm shells. We had stopped using the empty shell bags quite some time ago since they caused blockages. The warm shell cases would fall inside the driver's collar, being quite uncomfortable – I soon learnt that without a shirt they just bounced off my back without any problem. At this stage we were mostly barefoot, shirtless and wearing short pants.

'At one stage a mortar got stuck in the barrel and whilst Harry was trying to get it out I assisted Phillip (Roussow) by firing the Browning. The solenoid was not working and under normal circumstances Harry would pull the trigger while Phillip aimed by turning the turret. In this case I pushed the trigger from below – in a contact situation the driver did not have much else to do. Soon we had to pull back to the echelon to re-arm but returned immediately once bombed up again. Soon after 17.00hrs the battle was over – we walked to some of the FAPLA trenches and saw an abandoned recoilless gun with several enemy dead including a Cuban with a hole in his back. We moved further westwards into a mountain pass and slept on the road. It was raining and we pitched our lean-to tent on the road and made coffee inside. We slept uneasily that night not knowing what was waiting for us further up the road.'

In the first major battle of the advance so far, Jan Breytenbach affirmed: 'The captured documents indicated that we had been facing a regiment-sized unit, probably 1,000 men or more, plus their support weapons and crews as well as Cuban involvement at a senior level.'

Victory was achieved by a classic pincer movement undertaken by Battle Group Alpha with 5 Troop in support that set up an ambush on the road towards Benguela. One of the first 90mm shots struck an ammunition truck that exploded and in turn destroyed several other vehicles. At this point they also shot out a number of sedan vehicles transporting high-ranking officers and Cuban advisers fleeing the action, a not uncommon occurrence. The road to the vital port of Benguela was now open to Task Force Zulu.

In the event the town fell despite a concerted FAPLA artillery and rocket bombardment. 3 Troop arrived at Benguela airport at 11.00hrs on 6 November – Day 17 of Operation 'Savannah'. Benguela was a major objective as it was the main loading port for Zaire's export of copper. After a night spent on the beach, 3 Troop joined the advance on Lobito that was captured by Battle Group Alpha. Again many FAPLA troops fled northwards together with their Cuban advisers, but at a cost. With their growing confidence, Elands were positioned, sometimes as single vehicles, on the escape routes heading north.

In one such incident, Cpl Ben le Roux in Tango Four Five Alpha had adopted a 'turret-down' position behind the rise of a long straight road with a clear view of almost a mile. He then observed a yellow Datsun 1200 approaching at high speed. The vehicle contained one Cuban and three FAPLA officers. Crossing the brow of the hill, they saw the armoured car right in front of them. The vehicle's brakes were not too good and it stopped less than 10yd from the Eland. Corporal le Roux got halfway out of the hatch and calmly told them – in Afrikaans – that they must reverse, as he could not shoot with the main weapon at such a short distance.

Somehow they understood the instruction, selected reverse gear and careered backwards, losing control of the Datsun. Recovering, they turned the vehicle around, picking up speed. A moment later, a 90 HE round hit the rear of the Datsun. There were no survivors.

With further prevarication from Pretoria, Task Force Zulu was obliged to stay in Lobito for four frustrating days when the road to the capital of Luanda was clear and the deadline of 11 November looming. On that day the advance resumed towards Novo Redondo with 3 Troop attached to Battle Group Bravo in the wake of Battle Group Alpha. Because of the delay, FAPLA resistance was now stiffening with Battle Group Alpha subject to several concerted ambushes with Tango Four Five Alpha hit in the turret by an HE projectile, although the crew survived without serious injury. Tango Four One Alpha, commanded by Cpl Piet Swanepoel, was not so lucky when it was hit on the barrel by an RPG deflecting into the left mudguard before exploding by the right-hand door. Although the penetration was just 1cm in diameter, all three crewmembers were injured and the Eland had to be back-loaded to Rundu.

However, for 3 Troop the approach to Novo Recondo was less dramatic and more amenable. Sam van den Berg recalled:

'The next couple of days in Novo Redondo were most probably the highlight of the trip. It was a beautiful coastal town with an endless beach lined by palm trees. We were based in an open parking area between a large government building and a large hotel. The echelon took control over some very cheap wine. We were all issued with a bottle each. We quickly fetched some wine glasses from the government building and drank wine from these fine glasses. The quality of the wine, however, ensured heavy heads the next day but a swim soon cured any after-effects. The days were spent on patrols trying to find an alternative route over the Queve river, but at least the evenings were spent in comfort.'

Therein lay the problem. FAPLA and Cuban engineers were now mining and destroying all the road bridges over rivers that might impede the advance of the South Africans. The campaign was changing as Sam van den Berg observed:

'From Novo Redondo we travelled south towards Lobito then turned off towards Alto

Hama. We travelled in pouring rain and we arrived fairly late at Alto Hama. We moved into a hotel there after all; we became used to luxuries during our stay in Novo Redondo! The next morning we left for Cela where the whole nature of the operation changed. At Cela we noticed quite large numbers of SADF infantry and other armoured car troops, realising that the operation was, at least at this stage, much bigger than we had thought. During our time at Cela we did daily patrols and stayed in the veld. We were no longer attached to Battle Group Bravo and quite often operated alone.

'Cela is also a beautiful green area with black rock hills and farmlands everywhere. We were now in the middle of their rainy season and the terrain was very difficult for our heavy vehicles. We became used to the daily rain squalls and quite often used the opportunity to take a shower. If we were in a camp situation when the rain came we would take our clothes off and put them in the bins. We would just walk around naked in the rain. When the rain squall passed we would put our clothes back on fresh as a daisy.

'The roads were all red clay with a rounded surface and very slippery. If one did not exercise proper care it was easy to slip sideways off the road into the ditches at the sides. In such a case one just had to keep momentum with the front wheels turned as far as possible towards the road and hope for a place where the car could climb out. The fields were soggy from the rain and we had to steer clear of them so that we did not get stuck. There were also numerous wooden bridges over rivers and streams. We were informed of a large enemy build-up and of three armoured cars that had been shot out in quick succession. That was the first we heard about what later on became known as the Battle of Ebo.

'On the night of the 23rd (November) we were positioned at cross roads as a listening post. We were told not to engage FAPLA as a single troop and to withdraw if we noticed any enemy approach. On the 29th we were ordered back to Cela where we had to hand over our cars to replacement crews that were flown in. We then flew to Grootfontein by Flossie (C-130). For 3 Troop Operation "Savannah" was over. At the end of the day our confidence in the Eland

and our own ability really gave us the edge when engaging the enemy.'

The final word goes to a proud veteran of Operation 'Savannah', Basil Duke-Norris, a PF sergeant infantry instructor:

'What I can say as an infantryman during Operation "Savannah" is that those young boys manning the Eland armoured cars were harder and tougher than the steel that their Noddy Cars were made of. They demonstrated utmost bravery, determination, skill and zeal while leading the advance and on contact never faltered. The only time that a car withdrew from contact was to replenish ammo or evacuate casualties. The Eland did not have the off-road cross-country ability in wet and muddy conditions and a lot got bogged down, but they kept on fighting under very adverse conditions and gave the enemy hell. They led the advance under all conditions on the battlefield without infantry protection, as we had FNLA and UNITA troops who would just not deploy in front or alongside the Noddy Cars. These cars, although lightly protected against small arms fire only, never hesitated to take on the enemy. Their size and mobility was advantageous and the 90mm main armament, although restricted to 3,000m, was highly accurate and lethal with their 7.62mm Browning machine guns doing most of the work that infantry would have been expected to do. With each and almost every advance to contact, these little armoured fighting vehicles really proved their might and were manned and controlled by Boys of Steel. I salute them.'

BELOW The Eland enjoyed a long and distinguished career within the South African Armoured Corps, earning the enduring affection and esteem of its crews. With the inception of the South African Defence Force following the change of government in 1994, the Eland was withdrawn from service within the Permanent Force but continued with the Citizen Force for some years. Then, like the fate of so many AFVs, scores upon scores of perfectly serviceable Elands were condemned to destruction on the firing ranges: an ignominious end for such an outstanding armoured car.

Sources and bibliography

Sources

Panhard AML and Eland handbooks, Sentinel Projects, *Képi Blanc* magazine, *Paratus* magazine, *Shiryon* magazine, the archives of Rea Cullivan.

Bibliography

Colonel Jan Breytanbach, *The Buffalo Soldiers* (RSA, Galago, 1999)

El Escuadrón Olvidado: Panhard en Malvinas (Private Publication)

Christopher F. Foss, *Jane's Armour and Artillery 1988–89*, and *2000–01* (London, Jane's, 1988 and 2000)

Kyle Harmse and Simon Dunstan, *South African Armour of the Border War 1975–1989* (Oxford, Osprey, 2017)

Sir Roy Jackson, *The Hobby Horseman* (Private Publication, 2018)

Steve Camp and Helmoed-Römer Heitman, *Surviving the Ride* (RSA, 30° South Publishing, 2014)

Paul Moorcraft and Peter McLaughlin, *The Rhodesian War* (Barnsley, Pen & Sword, 1982)

Richard M. Ogorkiewicz, Design and Development of Fighting Vehicles (TSB, 1968)

Richard M. Ogorkiewicz, *Tanks – 100 Years of Evolution* (Oxford, Osprey, 2015)

Willem Steenkamp, *South Africa's Border War 1966–1989* (RSA, Ashanti, 1989)

Peter Stiff, *Taming the Landmine* (RSA, Galago, 1986)

Pierre Touzin, *Les Véhicules Blindés Français 1945 à nos jours* (EPA, 1976)

Francois Vauvillier, *The Encyclopedia of French Tanks and Armoured Vehicles 1914–1940* (Paris, Histoires & Collections, 2014)

David Williams, *Springboks, Troepies and Cadres* (NB Publishers, 2012)

David Williams, *On The Border 1965–1990* (RSA, Tafelberg, 2009)

Clive Wilsworth, *First In Last Out* (RSA, 30° South Publishing, 2010)

Steven J. Zaloga, *French Tanks of World War II (2)* (Oxford, Osprey, 2014)

Panhard AML specifications

Combat weight	4.5 tonnes (60)/5.5 tonnes (90)
Chassis weight	3.380 tonnes
Overall length	3.76m (60)/5.11m (90)
Overall height	1.91m (60)/2.07m (90)
Overall width	1.93m (60)/1.97m (90)
Ground clearance	0.33m
Crew	3
Panhard engine (4-cylinder flat)	90hp @ 4,300rpm
Range (road)	600km
Maximum speed (road)	90kmh
Fuel consumption (road)	25 litres/100km
Fording capability	1.10m
Vertical obstacle	0.30m
Onboard fuel (main + reserve = total)	150 litres + 6 litres = 156 litres
Oil tank	1.5 litres
Engine displacement	5 litres
Clutch	Centrifugal-type Gravina
Transmission	6AV/1AR
Hull armour	12mm to 30mm
Turret armour AML H60	8mm to 16mm
Turret armour AML H90	8mm to 15mm
60mm armament	60mm CS mortar
Direct-fire range	Max 300m
Indirect-fire range	From 200m to 1,600m
Ammunition capacity (60-7/60-7 command)	53/32
Ammunition capacity (60-1/60-12 command)	41/30
Co-axial armament (60)	
AML 60-7	2 x AA-52 (7.5mm)
Ammunition capacity (60-7/60-7 command)	3,800 rounds/3,200 rounds
AML 60-12	1 x 12.7mm M2HB
Ammunition capacity (12-7 rounds/12-7 command)	1,200 rounds/900 rounds
Weapon elevation (60mm)	
AML 60-7 (mg/mortar)	–15° – +60°/–15° – +76°
AML 60-12 (mg/mortar)	–11° – +76°/–11° – +76°
(90mm CN-90-F1)	90mm F1 (DEFA 921)
Effective range	1200mm
Ammunition stowage	20
Co-axial armament (H90)	1 x AA-52 (7.5mm)
Ammunition stowage	2,000 rounds
Elevation (90)	–8° – +15°
Wireless equipment (French Army)	
AML 60 (MA)	1 x ANVRC 10
AML 60 command (MA + MF)	1 x ANVRC 10 + 1 x ANGRC 9
AML 90 (MA)	1x ANVRC 10

Vehicle performance

- Maximum road speed 90kmh @ 4,700rpm
- 6th gear: 90kmh
- 5th gear: 61kmh
- 4th gear: 35kmh
- 3rd gear (off-road): 18kmh
- 2nd gear (off-road): 9.3kmh
- 1st gear (off-road): 4.5kmh
- Reverse: 5.5kmh
- 600km range on roads, or 15hrs
- 60% incline, 30% slope
- Amphibious capability without preparation. Speed in water 4kmh.

Index